I0084892

Beautiful Overcomer

Beauty can be birthed from the ashes of your life.

Sherry Lynn

SLF Publishing

Harrisburg, Pennsylvania

Copyright © 2017 by Sherry Lynn Weitzel

Edited by Jack Lynn.

All rights reserved. No part of this publication may be reproduced, distributed or transmitted in any form or by any means, without prior written permission.

Please note: SLF Publishing has made the stylistic choice to capitalize certain nouns and pronouns as pertaining to the Father, Son, and Holy Spirit.

Scripture quotations marked ESV are taken from the English Standard Version. Scripture quotations marked KJV are taken from the King James Bible. Scripture taken from THE MESSAGE. Copyright © 1993, 1994, 1995, 1996, 2000, 2001, 2002. Used by permission of NavPress Publishing Group. Scripture quotations marked TPT are taken from *Song of Songs: Divine Romance* or *The Psalms: Poetry on Fire,* The Passion Translation, copyright© 2014. Used by permission of BroadStreet Publishing Group, LLC, Racine, Wisconsin, USA. All rights reserved.

SLF Publishing
Harrisburg, PA 17111
www.sherrylynnfire.com/slf-publishing

Publisher's note: names have been removed to protect the identity of individuals.

Book Layout © 2017 BookDesignTemplates.com

Beautiful Overcomer, -- 1st ed.
ISBN 9780692921494

To my Tribe:
Membership is always open

Contents

Chapter 1

Why I Want You to Read This

D ear Overcomer, it is time to arise and shine for Him!

The pages of this book hold the invaluable lessons in overcoming that I have learned as a result of my time spent in the refining fire. It was here within the fire that the message of my messy life was discovered. Like you, I am just an ordinary individual following an extraordinary God. Little distinguishes me from any other believer; I am merely a woman who has walked through the fire and come out on the other side forever changed. I am a woman who, as a result, has been drawn closer to her Heavenly Father.

This is my story of the getting from here to there; getting from the fiery pit of trials to my breakthrough moment. It is a story birthed in beauty from ashes, and I share it in the hope that you might experience similar results. It is also my hope that, as you read this book, you will develop a greater understanding of who you are and to whom you belong. It is my prayer that you will learn to be more *you* while you grow closer to Him, always seeking more of Him as you become more of who He created you to be. May you find encouragement as you realize that you are not alone—that the Lord walks with you at all times. May you come to seek Him with all your heart, soul, and mind. May what is written within these pages be instrumental as you step into the fullness of the life He has planned for you. I hope these words, along with the message within them, equip and strengthen you for the battle in which you are engaged against an unseen enemy. May you find the courage to discover your passions and the motivation to follow your dreams, because until you do the world will be missing something that only you can bring. Just imagine what could be accomplished for the Kingdom if each of us stepped into our destinies!

As you follow your destiny-dreams—placed within your heart by the Father—I pray you reach your point of *enough,* no longer allowing those visions of a better world to remain hidden. That is my dream: to help you discover and pursue yours and, as you make this discovery, grow closer to God along the way. For too many years, I allowed my dream to remain hidden as I mistakenly believed I was not worthy enough to pursue it. It was deep within my crisis, my very moment of *enough,* that I realized it was time to move forward with my dream of helping the hurting individual who sat in the church pew week after week. You may recognize her as she faithfully serves in the nursery or teaches a Sunday School class. She may be the worship leader seen by all, or it may the newcomer who attends services every week, keeping her head down as she quickly scurries out of the church building Sunday after Sunday.

Regardless of who this person is, they all have one thing in common: they attend services while keeping a dark secret. Every one of these individuals, regardless of the façade they present to the rest of the world, is deeply wounded. Each week, they come looking for hope and healing, yet, week after week, they return home still wounded and weary. I understand this person because I was this person.

In my decision to take the pain of my trials and turn it into a ministry, I share my hard-learned lessons, lessons that may very well encourage you on your journey in personally discovering your amazing qualities. Along the way, I hope you also discover who you are in Christ and begin to carry yourself like the son or daughter of the King that you are. I want you to learn that you *can* do all things through Christ; that if He calls you, He will also equip you. You are here for a purpose, and it is time to discover what that purpose is. Most importantly, I want you to read this book so you might draw closer to Jesus; to come to know Him like you would a friend.

You have been placed on this earth for a reason, and, until you discover what that is, the world is missing something. I believe that you have been saved to do more than sit in a pew each Sunday. Rather than attempting to hide in your seat by remaining invisible, I want you to learn to give yourself permission to really be yourself. In Christ, you already have this permission to love, to overcome, to become, to be *you*. You have so much to offer and there is another budding overcomer just waiting to hear your story. As you read what is written in these pages, I pray you find your voice. Once you find it, fight to keep it; don't let the enemy silence you!

Overcomer, you may find yourself in tough times right now, but you can still experience the faithfulness of the Lord as the trials teach us who God is and wants to be for us. I share what I've learned in my trials so you can see how He has brought me through them so that you too can learn from my experiences. Those who have been through the fire recognize fellow firewalkers. These individuals walk out of the fire carrying buckets of hope which are then used to extinguish the flames surrounding their companions who remain in the fire.

In this season of testing and preparation I hope you can also learn to lean in as you allow God to do the necessary work on you. Learn that even in the midst of trials and tears, you possess the ability and the desire to praise Him. May you experience the same boldness and freedom that I have as you realize His love existed towards you before you ever even knew what it meant to be loved. May you release your fear of allowing others to see your humanness; release the need to be perfect; release whatever it is that might be holding you back from overcoming. May the goodness of a life lived for Him overshadow the darkness and challenges that this life can bring.

I must admit, I've learned my lessons the hard way, but it is also my prayer that your journey towards overcoming will be a little easier as a result of sharing my experiences. Will learning from my mistakes cause the trials to disappear from your life? No; sadly, trials will always be there, but this knowledge just might better equip you to fight the battle in which you are engaged.

Throughout my season in the fire, I often had opportunities to hear the testimonies of those who had walked through this season of refinement before me. As I listened, a question often arose concerning how to actually get from here to there. *How do I get to my finish line?* While this journey will remain unique for each of us, some truths are applicable to all. My goal is to guide you, getting you a little closer to that finish line as I share how the Lord has eased the hardships of the journey along the way.

My prayer is that, as a result of reading what is contained within these pages, you might grow in the Lord, or even find Him for the first time. It is also my prayer that you might be encouraged, that your heart is set on fire, your passions are ignited, and you set out in pursuit of your destiny. I've heard it said that believing in someone is one of the greatest gifts you can give them, so I will believe in you until you can believe in yourself. God loves you too much to let you stay where you are, and, as painful as this transition season may be, it is necessary in order to grow. While you walk through the fire, hold fast to His promises, continue to wait for that breakthrough—it might be just around the corner—and start overcoming so that you can begin living the life the Lord has for you. Then, use your breakthrough to set others free.

Although I walked through the most trying season of my life, I slowly realized I had a story to share that could set others free from bondage. So do you. We each have something unique to offer, but it just might require a wilderness journey to prepare you for your destiny. Don't wait until your life is perfect; start carrying the buckets of life-giving relief to your fellow firewalkers today. No matter how hot the fire burns, you can always offer encouragement—you will always have enough to give away.

Sons and daughters of the King—and that includes you!—conduct themselves like royalty. Applying this truth to your life will allow you to enter each situation life brings with the grace necessary to get you through as you glorify Him through your actions. Royalty acts confidently, walks with assurance in knowing who protects them, has no doubts about their authority, and expects preferential treatment. One phrase which I heard often throughout my season of overcoming was "for such a time as this" from the book of Esther. Like Esther, we are being prepared for that moment in which we discover our very reason for being, something we have been in training for our entire life. Unlike Esther, too many of us find the journey too difficult and give up before reaching this moment; nevertheless, I know you will continue on, because you are an overcomer.

To all of you beautiful overcomers: the potential within you is amazing. Scriptures remind us, "Arise, shine; for thy light is come, and the glory of the Lord is risen upon thee" (Isaiah 60:1, KJV).

Chapter 2

Because a Woman Prayed

Prayer; such a simple action, such amazing results. Which reminds me of the story of the woman with the alabaster box who poured the costly perfume on the feet of Jesus as found in Mark. One portion of Scriptures states, "She hath done what she could" (Mark 14:3, KJV), and it's one of my favorite phrases. We do what we can; we do what is within our power to do, such as praying. Because a woman prayed, the Lord called me to Him and I answered. Rarely do I get through my testimony without shedding a few tears over the beauty of this statement and all it has come to mean to me. To any of you who are praying for a loved one to come to the Lord; don't stop. Never give up until they have accepted Him as Savior.

In thinking back to my childhood, I realize that I've never doubted the existence of God, nor have I ever doubted the story of creation. When I was growing up, my mother took us to a Lutheran church, where I took the requisite confirmation classes, was involved in choir, and helped out with VBS.

Attending church was a pleasant experience, but I remember very little doctrine. What I do remember the most was an encouraging pastor who often responded to his flock with a heartening "Way to go!"

Then life changed.

When I was fifteen, my parents divorced and church became a distant memory from my early childhood. The years from fifteen to twenty-eight were spent in a haze created by alcohol. I'm not even sure why I began drinking and smoking at fifteen. Perhaps I did it as a result of peer pressure, or maybe I did it to hide the pain of not being enough; I was always not good enough in some way or another; not pretty enough, thin enough, or smart enough. Even though I can't tell you why I did these things, I can tell you that I allowed it to rule both my life and my decision making for far too long.

The fog of alcohol caused me to make a number of very poor choices, and, as a result, I carried around a lot of guilt and shame. I don't know if my shame was more or less than that of the average person, because I believe we all carry shame around in our bags from our past; our bags are simply packed differently. I ended up trying college, only to drop out; trying marriage, only to be hit once and only once before leaving; trying many jobs, but never finding the one that was right for me. In spite of all of my searching, I could never find the right fit in any area of life, and through it all, I continued to drink and make those poor choices.

Until one day, when I finally reached the bottom of the pit. I'd had enough of drinking, enough of waking up hung-over, and enough of my poor choices. After a particularly painful breakup from yet another bad decision, I decided I was done. This day proved to be a milestone in other ways as well, for it was here that I began to respond to a call I had been hearing. This call had yet to be defined, but still promised to fill that gaping hole within my soul.

I had been trying to fill that God-sized hole with anything that made me feel better for a moment; this included alcohol, relationships, shopping, and countless other ineffective fillers. But you can't fill emptiness with more emptiness. I decided I was finished with all of it. That tug in my heart led me on a search for the one thing that would fill this void in my life once and for all.

I looked at the lives of those around me whom I admired; friends who were married with children, had a stable home, seemed respectable, held on to jobs—all of the stable traits that had been missing in my own life. As I looked at their lives, I also began to ask questions. What made their lives different, or better, than mine? Why were they successful? What did they have that I didn't? Taking what I gathered from their lives, I attempted to create a more stable life of my own. I mistakenly believed the answer to the emptiness I was experiencing could be found in education, causing me to set a standard of perfection that was, in reality, unobtainable as I unsuccessfully attempted to earn what was missing from my life.

During this period of searching, a friend fixed me up on a blind date. That date turned into more dates, which then turned into a relationship, which eventually turned into a proposal and, ultimately, a marriage. Throughout the months we dated, I noticed he often went to church on Sundays. After some time had passed, I finally asked why he never invited me to accompany him. Guess where I went the next week?

In the course of my first Sunday of attending church, I experienced a type of culture shock. What was an altar call, anyways, and why would I want to walk the aisle in front of everyone? But I kept going, and I kept listening and as I listened, I also met a woman who I often chatted with before services. What first caught my attention was the manner in which the pastor spoke of the assurance you could have towards eternal life. This was a completely new concept to me, but I knew I wanted that! It took a few more sermons, a few more Sundays of me listening about the sinner in need of a Savior, before I realized the pastor was talking about me. I was that sinner; I was in need of a Savior! One Thursday evening in November, 1991, the pastor and a deacon visited my home and led me in a sinner's prayer. I accepted the Lord as my Savior, dedicated my life to Him, and things have never been the same since. A few weeks later, I participated in a believer's baptism, through which I publically demonstrated my decision to follow Jesus.

From day one of salvation, a fire was ignited in my heart; a fire which drove me to serve my Lord in any way I could. So I did. I put my time in the nursery, taught Sunday School, taught VBS, worked in Youth Group, worked in women's ministry, held Bible studies in my home, brushed up on my music skills to play piano and organ—poorly, but enthusiastically—even scrubbed toilets for a season. I had a willing heart to serve which also spilled over into my home life as I worked to be a godly wife to my husband and raise my children in the Lord.

Meanwhile, as life continued, my marriage suffered. I won't share many details here out of respect, but I cannot deny that my marriage got bad; undeniably, exceedingly bad. Living in our home became too dangerous, and I feared for the safety of my children and myself, finally reaching a point in which we had no other choice but to leave.

It was the most trying season of my entire life. A season that I didn't think I'd ever get through—and many times I didn't care whether or not I did. I experienced trial after trial: financial hits, spiritual attacks, issues with living arrangements, car problems—I could continue, but I imagine you get the idea. While all these trials were coming at me, something else was also occurring, and it was out of this season that my destiny was birthed.

Since the day of my salvation I knew that I was created to encourage others as they walked through the fire, to mine for the gold within them, to pull out their uniqueness, and to help them find their gifts and talents. It was in the midst of my existential crisis that I discovered my destiny was to help others discover their purpose. I longed to reach the hurting woman sitting in the pew week after week, knowing that, while she looked okay on the outside, inside she was barely holding on.

For the duration of my walk through the fire, I stored up all the lessons I had learned in hopes of one day encouraging others. As the fire burned away all the unnecessary lies and false beliefs, what resulted was pure gold. Much like a fire will burn away the impurities of gold, this fire was dealing with my past—particularly my guilt and shame—burning away the filthiness within me. Although I struggled to learn these lessons, I knew that I wasn't alone. Accompanying the newfound knowledge of each trial was also an increased desire to use it to help others.

So here I am. Occasionally the flames will burn a little hotter as more refining becomes necessary. I know this will be a lifelong journey. So here I am, sharing my testimony with you in hopes of encouraging you on your Jesus-walk. Here I am, Lord, use my story.

By now, you are most likely wondering what woman prayed what?

The woman I met at church—who was to become my mother-in-law—had watched each of her children marry except her eldest son. It was for him and his future wife that she prayed; I am forever thankful for her prayers as it is through them that the Lord began His work in my heart, through her prayers the lure of alcohol lost its power, and through her prayers the voice of the Lord called to me and I answered. For that, I am forever thankful!

If you've never met the Lord on a personal basis, please read the section on salvation. Who knows, there may be someone praying for you right now. I can't wait to hear your testimony!

Chapter 3

Why We Tell Our Story

When was the last time you shared your story with someone? Too many of us fail to realize how much sharing our story can encourage another on their journey towards overcoming. We allow our voices to be silenced when we should be telling the world what Jesus has done for us by shouting from the rooftops. Do you think you have nothing to share? Take a moment and look back over your life. You've already overcome quite a bit, haven't you?

There are many reasons to share our stories. One reason to reveal our history is so that we might brag about what Jesus has done in our lives. We are reminded in Scriptures, "Come and hear, all ye that fear God, and I will declare what he hath done for my soul" (Psalm 55:16, KJV). The Lord has done great and mighty things in my life, and, while I may not be a mighty woman, I am a woman of a mighty God. What He has done, is doing, and will do in the future is worth conveying, as each of my trials has prepared me to minister to another hurting brother or sister in the Lord.

While we are boasting about what Jesus has done for us, others will most likely become free from what binds them. Our stories offer comfort and encouragement as they tell of others who have already travelled this uncharted territory; this encouragement is reserved not only for the listener, but for the teller of the tale as well. As you communicate your story, you too will be lifted up as you look back at the path traveled, noticing how far the Lord has brought you.

I imagine you are already forming your argument against the need for sharing your testimony, basing it on your worth, reminding me of all the mistakes you have made along the way, all your sins, all your humanness. I hear you; I presented those very same arguments when faced with the choice to share my story. My life didn't turn out as expected–does anyone's? We can either decide to remain quiet or we can openly share what the Lord has done. Work diligently to find your voice and craft your tale as you determine to impart the wisdom you have learned through trial and error in your own life. The Lord knew you would end up exactly where you are in this moment, but all along the way He was preparing you to use your pain to help others, using each trial to teach you a specific lesson.

Keep in mind: the ultimate goal of the enemy is to keep us from our destiny and to keep us from advancing the Kingdom of the Lord as he keeps us so distracted that we never discover our purpose. I humbly, and ashamedly, admit his tactics have worked all too well on me as, at times, I have allowed his lies to distract me from God's call. Even as I write this book I struggle with the value of what I have to say through my story. Dear overcomer, we need to fix our eyes on what God has called us to do and not stop until we have achieved it! Stop worrying about all the *what ifs* and start concentrating on your radical obedience to follow the Lord. You have been prepared for such a time as this!

Interwoven amongst our individual stories is an even greater one: a story filled with Kingdom promises, complete with an overarching theme of the Lord's trustworthiness and love towards us. Too many of us sit in the church pew week after week silently screaming for help as the pain of life threatens to overwhelm. Too often these same individuals don't share their story or allow another to walk beside them as they experience life. This needs to stop. Take a chance and share your account of what the Lord has done in your life. Yes, you might get hurt a few times, but it is worth the pain when you can help just one person. You may find that as you make your story public, you are not walking this path alone as you find fellow overcomers along the way.

During the course of your journey, you may often feel as if the season you are in is threatening to destroy you and silence your voice. Through it all, continually turn to the Lord and He will sustain you, providing for your every need. One day, you will experience a lull in the attacks of the enemy, and, when you do, you will notice that you really have come a long way. You might not be where you want to be, but you also aren't where you once were. The tears and struggles may still be there, but along the way you have developed a newfound strength, one that is firmly founded on the Lord. As eyes are opened and awareness increased, we begin to see more and more of what the Lord is doing in our life, noticing He truly is on our side as He works all things together for our good (Romans 8:28). Life may not look as expected but God is still faithful in His provision and that too is a story worth sharing.

Accompanying this discovery is the realization that everything the enemy is throwing at you in his attempt to destroy you is only making you stronger. The journey is not an easy one, and, if we had our choice, we would take a different path; but throughout the entire journey, we grow. Trust grows, faith grows, and even your love towards the Lord grows in the trials as you develop a closer relationship with Him. Remind yourself that the very Creator of the universe is with you as He fights your battles for you, preparing the way before you.

I can already hear your argument. *But I'm not worthy. My story isn't worth sharing. Who am I?* Your arguments are pointless because, with God, the broken can be made whole; with God, the mess can turn into a message; and, with God, beauty can be found within the ashes. That's why I encourage you to share your story; it most likely isn't pretty and it may not be very extraordinary, but it is yours to tell.

As you share your story with others, the goal is to showcase Him; this journey is all about developing a deeper, more intimate relationship with the Lord. You might need to share your story a few times before you become comfortable as a storyteller, and that's perfectly okay. You will most likely make mistakes, and that's okay too; the Lord can use your less than perfect story because, buried deep within the ashes of your life, there are hidden facets of beauty waiting to be discovered and shared. We've all made mistakes and done things we aren't proud of. I'd guess we all hide those things as well. Rather than allow these events to remain hidden, use the power of your testimony and the blood of Jesus as you battle against the enemy. Our words wield great power; as we use them to take down the enemy, we can also build up a brother or sister in the Lord, reminding me of the verse, "And they overcame him by the blood of the Land, and by the word of their testimony" (Revelation 12:11, KJV).

Another reason to share your story is because we are commanded to. The Great Commission reminds us, "Go ye therefore, and teach all nations, baptizing them in the name of the Father, and of the Son, and of the Holy Ghost: Teaching them to observe all things whatsoever I have commanded you: and, lo, I am with you always, even unto the end of the world. Amen" (Matthew 28:19-20, KJV). In the course of sharing the Gospel, our story becomes so intertwined with His story that the two cannot be separated. When you tell others about Jesus, you cannot help but contribute to the story, adding what He has done in your life and how He has changed you.

Because of this, I encourage you to share your story. Share with whoever will listen as you communicate how the Lord has revealed a previously untapped strength buried deep within you. Tell how He has pulled you out of the fiery pit and made you a new creation. Let others know how He has made a way when there was no way.

An old hymn came to mind as I was writing this chapter, written by H. Ernest Nichol: We've A Story to Tell to the Nations, the lyrics go as follows:

> We've a story to tell to the nations,
>
> That shall turn their hearts to the right,
>
> A story of truth and mercy,
>
> A story of peace and light.

Take a deep breath as you step out in faith telling your story of mercy, peace, and light, I know it's going to be amazing!

Chapter 4

From Religion to Relationship

Yay, it's Sunday and we get to go to church! Wow, I can't wait to read my bible today! Hallelujah, I can take all my worries to the Lord and leave them at His feet!

Is this you? Are you ecstatic over your relationship with the Lord? Have you ever asked yourself why you attend church? Do you go out of duty because we are not to forsake this type of assembly (Hebrews 10:25, KJV) or do you attend services because it's something you've always done? Maybe this attitude doesn't stop at the mandatory church attendance, either. Is your faith life as dry as the desert as you drag your feet, making little clouds of dust as you walk? Is your very soul parched and weary from the journey?

Overcomers, it doesn't have to stay that way.

Getting from religion to relationship is all about developing your love for Jesus. When something exciting happens in your life, who is the first person you look forward to sharing that news with? Who is your BFF that you tell all to? This may sound oversimplified, but a relationship with you is exactly what the Lord is looking for. He doesn't want you going through the motions, He wants all of you; including your heart. He wants your worship to be real and your prayers to be genuine and heart-felt as nothing less will do.

So often, we allow those few inches between our head and our heart to hold us back from all the Lord has for us. Remember when I mentioned I had never doubted the existence of God when sharing my testimony? There is a vast difference between knowing He exists and knowing *Him*. We may know something to be true, but until we experience that truth for ourselves, the knowledge between our head and our heart do not combine.

That is exactly the reason we need to get away from religion and into a relationship with Jesus. Unfortunately, too many believers go for years without ever stumbling upon this truth, but, for an overcomer, a personal experience—along with a personal relationship—with Jesus will take faith from religion into relationship. Get your head out of it and your heart into it! Logic has no use in your faith-walk so stop searching for a rational explanation to be found in the promises of God. Stop letting your head push you towards earning that free gift of salvation and let your heart simply accept it. Stop letting your head hold you back as you give your heart free reign to run after a relationship with the Lord.

Here are some of the differences between the two. Think of all your friendships, don't they require time spent together in order to cement the friendship? Doesn't a relationship require honesty, transparency, mutual respect, and more? God isn't calling to your brain, He's calling to your heart. Religion is cold, performance-based, and impersonal, while relationship is vibrantly growing as it allows for an authentic connection with the Creator. Religion imprisons us as we robotically go through the motions, while relationship brings new and exciting things each day. Religion raises concerns over imagined wrongs and fears as it asks questions such as: *Is any sin unforgivable?* Or, *will God turn away from me because of something I've done?* Relationship assures you He will never leave you or forsake you (Hebrews 13:5, KJV). Religion calls for perfection while relationship allows you to be flawed. Religion is Sunday mornings and Wednesday evenings, while relationship is first thing when you wake and last thing before you sleep—along with every moment in between.

I walked with the Lord for nineteen years before coming to this realization. It took a season in the fire to burn away all those false beliefs that kept me from experiencing Him. I discovered I didn't need to earn the privilege of worshipping the Lord, I could simply offer my praise resting in the knowledge that it would be accepted. Much like the Hebrews of the Old Testament—which you can read about in the Pentateuch—I approached my religion under a set of laws that were impossible for me to uphold.

But it is often in our lowest moments that we meet Him, often for the very first time, as we allow our defenses to fall. By allowing Him to see us as we truly are—all the shame, all the guilt, and all the imperfections—we learn just how much He loves us and we love Him. For it was here, in the pit, that I met Him in my vulnerability, allowing Him to see me as I was. As we move from a head knowledge to a heart knowledge, we are reminded that His amazing grace enables us to dispel every lie of the enemy—an enemy who takes the tiniest amount of truth—that we are not worthy of His love—and twists it around until we believe that we are *unable to be* loved. Our unworthiness does not mean we cannot be loved, it just means we cannot earn that love. While all have fallen and come short of God's glory (Romans 3:23, KJV), the only action required of us is accepting the love as it is offered.

In order to move from religion to relationship—from head to heart knowledge—decisions must be made, and they aren't always easy ones. Many are often tempted to turn their back on the Lord in order to make the trials stop, and, again, there is just the right amount of truth mixed into this lie. If the enemy can get us to take our eyes off of Jesus, we lose our effectiveness, and, while quitting is among your options, it is never the choice you want to make. You need to decide for yourself that you are not turning your back on the Lord and that you are choosing to put your faith in Him no matter what you may see in the natural.

I will admit, I struggled with this many times, even though I knew within my soul that this would never truly be an option. It was during one of these tests that I noticed something new and different: as a result of my choices, I was experiencing a more authentic, more intimate relationship with God as I gained experiential knowledge.

That space between my head and my heart was bridged as the knowledge I had *believed* to be true became knowledge I *knew* to be true. I never doubted for one moment that I loved Him, but I will admit there were a few times when I doubted that He loved me due to the circumstances in my life. Even though I was learning, I was still basing God's love towards me on performance and religion, as, all too often, I forgot I could do nothing to earn His love.

For years, I had read the verses on how much God loved me—as I imagine you have—and I believed them—to an extent. While I freely acknowledge that it was love that kept Him nailed to the cross as He gave His life for my sins, something within me was still holding onto religion. I believed He cared about me, I believed His promises were true, I even believed He loved me and wanted what was best for me as He worked things out for my good, but what I didn't believe was that these promises were mine to claim. For too long I had lived thinking that nothing I ever did was good enough, mistakenly believing there was always another hoop to jump through or another test in which to prove my worthiness. I failed to realize that my righteousness was like filthy rags (Isaiah 64:6, KJV).

My world changed once I realized I could never earn His approval—I didn't need to and I could stop trying. One of my favorite Scriptures, found in 1 John, says, "We love him because he first loved us" (4:19, KJV). Before we even knew what love was, the Lord had been there, loving us the entire time. The revelation of this love created a snowball effect in my life as lie after lie was replaced with truth. Along with this, my faith was being rebuilt from the ground up, this time with a cornerstone firmly anchored in Christ as I experienced His love firsthand. The second defining moment came when I realized that I was never going to reject Him either; I was never going to abandon Him or walk away. Throughout my trials, I uttered many prayers consisting of *don't let me walk away... don't let me turn my back on you, Lord.* These prayers were usually whispered frantically in the midst of an attack from the enemy, in my weakest moments, or in the darkest nights.

Looking back, I can remember examining my life only to make a startling discovery: even though I knew my righteousness was just filthy rags, some small part of me was still trying to earn the privilege of being loved by the Lord. I took great care in what I watched, read, and listened to, and worked diligently to forgive those who had offended me. I was doing everything right, everything I was supposed to be doing— or was I?

There is absolutely nothing wrong with doing any of those things. In fact, they are all good practices. The question comes down to motive. Perhaps it wasn't so much about what I was doing; isn't that religion? Everything I was doing was performance-based, as if I could earn my entrance into heaven one day. Let me be clear on this: while I completely believe the Lord enjoys our obedience to Him as well as our efforts to please Him, I believe He is also looking for something a bit different. He was looking not at what I was doing for Him, but why I was doing it. He was examining the reasons behind my actions; looking at my inward motivation rather than my outward robotic response. Our Heavenly Father looks for motive that is heart-based, for that is where we move from the cold, empty efforts of religion into an exciting, genuine connection with Him.

This connection is exactly what the Lord is looking for from all of us; a connection based on love. Along with that love comes a freedom to completely be yourself in the same way He is Himself with you. He truly does want to be your friend, your buckler, your shield and strength! He really is a very jealous God and would have no other gods or idols before Him. Scriptures remind us, "And thou shalt love the LORD thy God with all thine heart, and with all thy soul, and with all thy might" (Deuteronomy 6:5, KJV). He gives us free will to choose as we want, but being all-in with our relationship with Him is what He most desires.

As this truth becomes firmly embedded in both heart and brain, the overcomer will discover what a relationship with the Lord looks like. Comforting verses will take on new meaning as they are read from the perspective of relationship. As the words become more than words and the intent behind them becomes tangible, and as lies are replaced with truths, Scripture becomes little love notes sent by a loving Heavenly Father. Eyes become focused on Him; He becomes your hope as you enter a loving relationship with the One who sent His very son to die on the cross for you.

Tears and trials may continue, but now you take your concerns directly to your Heavenly Father, speaking to Him as you would your dearest friend. This behavior brings about a transformation as you develop a heavenly perspective, viewing all of life as He does, from a stance of victory, allowing you to firmly believe in the promises of God. Words that seemed just words now carry loving messages sent by your Heavenly Father.

At some point, you may have an opportunity in which you are able to look up from your trials as you experience an illuminating moment. Maybe there is a purpose to them; maybe, just maybe, all these trials are teaching you something. While God was using them to refine you, He was also reinforcing the message of His faithfulness. He won't abandon you like so many others have done in your past, nor will He reject you. He wanted you to know He was going to remain right where He was, by your side. While all this turmoil was occurring around you, He was allowing you to experience His love as He took you from religion to relationship.

Overcomer, when you arrive at this point of assurance, you will be free to seek and serve Him in entirely new and different ways as your motivation now comes from a heart bursting with love towards Him. This love spills over to others as it is fashioned out of abundance as a result of your relationship with Him. You might not fully understand this love, but it is one you can trust as you learn to lean on Him. It may be a love that does not look as expected, and that is okay too; trust that He knows what's best for you. You may also experience a glimpse of eternity as you sit at His feet enjoying tender moments of praise and worship originating from a heart overflowing with love towards Him, secure in the knowledge He will be with you always. That's relationship.

Moving from religion to relationship causes additional discoveries to be made. One is the inextinguishable flame of love towards your Lord that now burns brightly within your heart. In those moments when little seems good in your, life, you can trust that this flame will continue to illuminate your path in the deepest of darkness. When all that surrounds you is distorted and confusing, that flame will guide you directly towards Jesus.

As this flame guides them, overcomers realize they *need* Jesus. In a way, our Jesus-walk is that simple. He's not something or someone we get out on a Sunday or just visit on occasion, He is an integral part of our day from the time we wake up until the time we fall asleep, along with every minute in between. We don't have the luxury of only bringing Him out when we want to, we *need* to invite Him into every moment of our lives. That's relationship.

Often, this turning point from religion to relationship occurs in a crisis as that is where you must choose to believe that His love is personal and intimate. In your defining moment you must decide to allow Jesus to become real; to become more than a concept or a man who lived thousands of years ago. Finally, after nearly twenty years of being one of His followers, I came to believe this truth: I believed in His love towards me was exactly that, *towards* me and *for* me. He gave His life for you, and, regardless of what you may be faced with, you need to decide to live for Him. Make the decision to trust what you cannot see, choose to trust the promises as found in Scriptures. Live your life believing that when He was on the cross, you were on His mind. As long as—or rather because—there is breath in your lungs, praise Him until there is no breath left, then praise Him for all eternity as you spend it in His presence. He alone deserves your honor and praise; He alone is worthy of it all!

Once you experience relationship, you learn that there is always someone walking through the trials with you. Like Shadrach, Meshach, and Abednego in the third chapter of Daniel, because of His presence you will come out of the fire not even smelling of smoke, yet forever altered by the experience. God has your back. He is your best friend and will remain so for all eternity. As an overcomer, you will develop an affectionate relationship with the very Creator of the universe. As a result, the emptiness within your soul, the one that you have attempted—and failed—to fill with everything from food to shopping to alcohol has now been filled. You will never walk alone again, and you rest secure in that knowledge.

So often, religion has made the salvation experience complex, when all you really need is a child-like faith as you approach the Savior with love. Come to Him in faith, believing that He alone can save you from the punishment of your sins.

The clear, sweet Gospel message of His love will overwhelm you as it brings you to your knees with a love from Him that defies explanation; a love *from* Him that causes us to experience such a great love *for* Him. There are no words to describe the experience. That is relationship.

He loves me, I love him. That basically sums the relationship up. He died for our sins on the cross, and, while He hung there in agony, His thoughts were on each of us individually. We confess our sins, accept Him as savior, and those sins become covered by the blood of Jesus; this acceptance grants us the freedom to not just be the person we were created to be, but has a multitude of additional freedoms accompanying it. Freedom to love others, to step into our destiny, and to love and worship Him as never before. Learn to completely rely on Him as you willingly submit your life to Him, trusting Him with your future. Do not settle for less than His very best. As you reach the end of yourself, surrender to Him in safety, allowing Him permission to mold you into His image.

My advice: keep it simple! Get out of your head and let your heart run free, right into His arms. He's waiting patiently. Don't overthink or intellectualize—just believe. Silence the negative voices in your head as you remove your need for logic. Focus on what He says about you; find out who He is and what He is like for yourself.

Remember, He wants to be first in your life with no other gods before Him. Psalms remind us "You are the only God to be worshipped, for there is not a more secure foundation to build my life upon than you" (18:31b, TPT). Because of the love that nailed Christ to the cross, we see that God is always inviting us into a more familiar relationship with Him. Take a breath as you accept His invitation, let go of your religion, and step into a relationship with the Father.

Chapter 5

Learning to be Loved

He loves me; he loves me not; he loves me…how many of you recited that little ditty as a child, wondering if your crush returned your affections? God always loves you; of that there is no doubt—He loved you before you ever even gave Him a thought (Jeremiah 1:5). Scriptures remind us of this truth often because it's something many of us struggle with. But we never have to worry if He loves us or how much He loves us because we are completely loved by the Lord. In fact, He loves us so much that He sent His only Son to die on the cross for our sins. There is nothing you can do to lose His love, nor is there anything that can separate you from His love. We learn in Romans 8:39 (KJV), "Nor height, nor depth, nor any other creature, shall be able to separate us from the love of God, which is in Christ Jesus our Lord". No matter how hard we may try, we can never hide from His love either; He will always find us.

Due to past wounds, we may find ourselves fearful of accepting not only the love of others, but also the love of our Heavenly Father. Because I knew I was so flawed, on countless occasions I almost lost my way as I tried to push Him away; my finite mind was unable to comprehend how the Lord could love someone as damaged as I was. As I was refusing His love, He was constantly, peacefully, patiently waiting for the moment I could accept it. One of my favorite books of the Bible is Song of Solomon in the Passion Translation. It is here that God's words of love became real to me as they trickled down into all the cracked and broken places of my heart, providing much needed healing. In the first chapter, we see the Shulamite woman preparing to join her Shepherd-King; she speaks of how wonderful her groom-to-be is, but then she doubts her own worth. He—the Lord—reassures her, not just once but twice, of His love as He speaks these words: "Yet you are so lovely!" (Song of Songs 1:5b, TPT) as he counters her protestations. Just rest there for a moment and soak in those words. We desperately long for His love, yet, when He gives it, we put our hands up as if to cover our face to remind Him that we are unworthy. And yet, He remains. And yet, He finds us lovely!

It truly humbles me to realize that I am His beloved. I am deeply flawed and entirely imperfect, but, when my Lord looks on me, He sees only my potential. In spite of all my flaws—or maybe even because of them—my Heavenly Father loves me beyond measure. Today I know the love of the Lord, but it wasn't always that way.

For years I wandered through life with a cracked and broken heart, attempting to fill the gaping wounds with innumerable useless things, but you can't fill emptiness with more emptiness. There is only One who can fill the void: God. Only His love can bring the healing we all so desperately need.

Finally, after reaching the deepest point of the abyss, I learned how much He valued me. It was at the bottom of that slimy pit where I finally learned it was not necessary to *earn* His adoration; I didn't have to do or be anything special, didn't have to achieve greatness, didn't have to perform or be perfect. Slowly, I learned how to be treasured as the Lover of my Soul whispered His words of love in my ear. The knowledge that I was worthy of His adoration—or, rather, didn't have to be worthy of anything—released me from the performance trap in which I had been ensnared. How amazing it was to learn how He loved me before I even knew what it meant to be loved! Gone was the mentality that I had to do something that was always just out of my reach in order to receive that love; all I needed to do was invite Him in.

Many overcomers have lived a lifetime of rejection as a result of receiving countless messages of their worthlessness. For these individuals, learning to be loved can be difficult. Even once we have found Him, learning to fully accept what He is offering may take time. There is nothing that we can do to earn His love, it just has to be accepted as the gift it is. Overcomers can take all the messages of rejection and abandonment that they have received throughout their lifetime and relabel them "return to sender", refusing to allow these feelings to affect them any longer. One of my favorite quotes by Joseph Conrad sums this concept up quite nicely: "The cave you fear to enter holds the treasure you seek". What we want the most also terrifies us the most; it is a basic need of every human to be loved and accepted, yet, because of sin, we find this acceptance to be the most difficult to receive.

Face it: we are flawed, we have sinned, and we are unworthy of God's affection, yet He loves us anyway because He views us from a heavenly perspective. He sees us as we can be. It is challenging to learn to see yourself as God sees you: worthy of His love. You are perfectly imperfect and that is perfectly okay in His eyes. In order to overcome, it is necessary to recognize and accept the love of God. When the Father looks at you, He doesn't see all your sins and shortcomings; rather, He sees you as He created you to be. When He looks at you, the blood of Jesus covers your faults and imperfections, allowing God to see only the good attributes that mirror His own; all the gold that had been tarnished by sin has been polished and refined by the fiery trials through which we all walk. The Father sees us as we can be. He sees all the potential that lies dormant.

Just as you learn to be loved, you will also need to accept love from others. Life will require that you let others in so that you might benefit from community, friendship, and relationship with both your Heavenly Father and your fellow overcomers. As you combine your ability to be loved with an increase in trust, a new approach to life will become available to you as you conduct yourself as the child of the King that you are. As you discover who you are in Christ, you will become crazy about a

God who is crazy about you; an attitude of adoration that flows in both directions. For the overcomer who has come to learn to see themselves as God sees them, His love cannot help but spill over into the lives of others as you, in turn, begin to see as the Father sees.

When you learn you are loved, and that His thoughts towards you are for your good and not your destruction, you can accept the trials that come into your life with a different attitude. You will view others differently when you view them in love; you'll see yourself differently as well. The chains which once confined you are broken off as you realize you are cherished; the realization that you are worth loving and that you have been bought with a high price allows you to love others from an overflowing heart.

Learning that you are loved may not happen overnight; for most of you, each day will be a conscious choice to believe that you are worthy of that love and to believe in God's words of love as found in Scripture. We can rest in the knowledge that God has our best interests in mind; "For I know the thoughts that I think toward you, saith the Lord, thoughts of peace, and not of evil, to give you an expected end" (Jeremiah 29:11, KJV).

Your experience with freedom, as found in His love, will cause the enemy to have less and less of a hold over you. Of course, the enemy doesn't want us to know this, because without the ability to live in the Father's love, we are ineffective—which is exactly what he wants. Once we know that we are loved, we begin to walk in Kingdom authority, and that terrifies the enemy. Walking in this loving authority allows you to walk boldly and with great confidence in who God is for you. Once you learn that you are loved your focus will shift from inward to outward. Here you experience being a new creation, as stated in Scriptures: "Therefore we are buried with him by baptism into death: that like as Christ was raised up from the dead by the glory of the Father, even so we also should walk in newness of life" (Romans 6:4, KJV).

Not only does the Father love us, He continually reminds us of that love throughout the day in little love notes sent by Him. I'm sure you've experienced them without realizing what they were; maybe there was the song with the perfect message that came on the radio as you were driving to work, or maybe just the right Scripture came across your Bible reading. Many times, we find ourselves begging the Lord to speak to us only to discover that He has been sending messages all along the way and we were just missing them. His love notes are everywhere and can be received at any time. You will find them more often as your awareness increases.

I believe, without a doubt, that the greatest source of God's love notes is His Word. I suggest writing verses down and posting them wherever they can be seen. I also believe in hiding God's word in my heart and my favorite way to do this is by memorizing Bible passages. Put His word everywhere you look so you can see it each day; make it a part of your life, firmly embedded within your mind, claiming it as truth as you apply it to your life. For the overcomer, these words will illuminate the direction you need to take; they will encourage you as they rebuild your hope on those battle-weary days, and they will remind you of His affection towards you. Look for these love notes, anticipate them, expect to receive them, actively search for them, and purposefully set time apart to spend in His presence through music, Scriptures, or simply sitting at His feet. Look for them every day in every way, and learn to love yourself as one of God's creation as you do. Do not reject what God accepts; learn to accept yourself because God accepts you. Those same loving words of encouragement you would offer a friend also need to be offered to yourself, as oftentimes the grace we need to extend is to ourselves. Pray, prepare, and position yourself to receive these words along with the messages of love concealed within. Cherish these love notes, because your Heavenly Father authored them. When you receive these notes, speak the words contained within them over yourself. Ask Him for more of them, and then, when you receive them, don't cast them aside; pray into their message for greater revelation as you ask for understanding of the relevance these words have in your life.

As a beautiful overcomer learning to be loved, you must accept yourself as you are here and now. Don't wait until someday when life is perfect—it never will be. See yourself as that priceless treasure that Jesus died on the cross for. Realize you are not required to stay this way, and work to get rid of any insecurity that hinders your ability to receive love from others. Improve those things you don't like about yourself; acknowledge them, face them, and then deal with them. Remember, this love—the one from the Lord—doesn't care about who you are or what you do, but, rather, is focused on to whom you belong.

Throughout my journey I've learned some things about being loved by my Heavenly Father; here are a few. First and foremost—and perhaps most difficult—when the Lord tells you something, believe it is true. When He tells you that you are loved, take Him at His word; when He tells you He finds you lovely, you need to believe Him. Something similar would apply to your prayers; as you pray them, believe they will be answered to your benefit because of His love towards you. Keep in mind, both God and love are incapable of being confined to a box, if you've put either in one, release them and set them free. This truth ties into love not being logical; it isn't, nor does it need to be. By now, I imagine you are saying *but, but, but...but God*; yes, but God. He is the God of the impossible. He is the God whose love can break the chains and set you free. His love has such a pull that it can keep us close to Him as we continue to follow Him even in the trials. With God and His love, there is always enough and we can always bless another even when we are hurting. This same love will cast out any fear, allowing us to proceed with confidence as we stand firm in any situation, knowing we are loved. Jesus' love is so great for us that it kept Him nailed to the cross.

His love certainly does get us through the rough patches of life, and there is something else to keep in mind: there will also be times when God expresses His love differently than you might expect, often in the form of answering prayers in a way we might not agree with. I believe we receive answers to our prayers all the time but fail to notice them because they don't look like we were expecting them to look. But regardless of what those answered prayers look like—expected or unexpected—one thing will always hold true: from beginning to end, God's love towards you will never change. Trust Him to get you through; His love won't let you down, and you can live life loved because of that.

Chapter 6

Journey Toward Trust

Your heavenly Father holds out His hand in an invitation to you, requesting that you join Him on the journey of a lifetime; a journey which will lead to you trusting Him completely and to being accepted fully by Him as you develop an inspiring, contagious faith. The trust He calls you to is deceptively simple; just like a child inexplicably trusting their earthly father, so are we to trust our Heavenly Father.

All relationships require trust in order to progress towards greater intimacy; your relationship with your Heavenly Father is no different. A journey towards trust will increase this intimacy, enabling you to step out in faith more often as you come to the place in which your trust issues are dealt with and relegated to your past. The process of learning to trust can be likened to a mountain range; the climb up the mountainside doesn't happen all at once. Much like climbing a mountain, you will reach various heights depending on your skill level, and each successful climb will increase your climbing expertise. One day, you will look back with pride and realize how very far you've come on this trek.

At the beginning of this expedition, trust may be one of the biggest mountains to climb, as we've all been wounded at some point or other in our lives. Many of us may find ourselves struggling with trust because life hasn't worked out as expected, or prayers have not been answered in the way we desired. When that occurs, we become the walking wounded, in desperate need of healing as we, hurting people, continually hurt others. But in order to experience healing as offered by our Lord, we must first learn to trust.

Often what is directly in front of you, that which you can see with your eyes, looks impossible to overcome. It may be the mountain of addiction, a failed relationship, unemployment— any number of obstacles may be prohibiting your upward progression. In the natural, there appears to be no way to get from here to there, but remember, we serve a God of the impossible. What looks impossible to you and I is nothing to Him. As we develop the ability to view all of life from the perspective of the cross and its accompanying victory, we will find ourselves stepping out in faith more and more often. As these trust muscles are stretched, we will learn, without fail, that our God is worthy of our trust.

I have actually questioned if I must be a certain kind of stubborn as this was a lesson that I endured over and over again in my life. Due to the wounds and scars of my past, I found letting go of control and trusting another to be one of the most difficult assignments on my Jesus-walk. The same goes for trusting His promises. When my life was a mess, as days, weeks, and even years went by, trusting His promises became increasingly difficult. But trust is something we all must learn. We are reminded in Scriptures to "Trust in the LORD with all thine heart; and lean not unto thine own understanding" (Proverbs 3:5, KJV). I still don't understand my trials, but I have come to trust the lessons He has taught me as a result of them.

But how do we trust what we cannot see? The answer is both simple and complex. We increase our trust by taking a chance that maybe, just maybe, God's promises are true and applicable to us. We may stick our toes in the water to test it out, or we may prefer to jump right in, completely immersing ourselves in this voyage towards trust. Perhaps the greatest example of trust is a child; think of how completely they trust their parents. That is exactly how we are to trust our Heavenly Father.

Throughout my journey, I have learned that I do not have to know how I'm going to get from here to there, from where I currently find myself to where God wants me to be, despite my tendency towards planning and dreaming and expecting things to turn out a certain way. I don't have to be concerned with all of the details of how the promise is coming, I merely need to trust that He knows. It's taken multiple trials for me to learn this, but I finally understand that God's got me. It really is that simple: He's got me and He isn't letting go. The following verse really brought that home to me as the concept was worded so simply yet clearly in the following passage: "This one thing I know: God is on my side!" (Psalm 56:9, TPT). In another Psalm, we are reminded "God, you're such a safe and powerful place to hide! You're a proven help in time of trouble; more than enough and always available whenever I need you" (Psalm 46:1, TPT).

I've also learned that even when I don't understand, or particularly *when* I don't understand, He does and there is no cause for concern. Things will work out. Worrying changes nothing. For a planner like me, conquering my trust issues was huge! In fact, it is still a battle that I fight on occasion. I've learned to remind myself to take baby steps, because this journey towards trust will likely take a lifetime.

On this quest, remember to extend yourself the very same grace and kindness that you would a friend. Encourage yourself to celebrate each and every victory in which you let go of your control and allowed God to be God. This is a daily choice as we choose to believe His word, exercising faith as we believe what we cannot see. Remembering how God has proven Himself trustworthy throughout past trials can cause the journey to become smoother in the present. When I look back over my own journey towards trusting, I had to wonder how I could fail to trust Him when His track record was one of continued provision. Time and again He would provide, proving it was safe to put my trust in Him, but time and again I found myself worrying about how life was going to unfold. I had to make a conscious choice to leave my worries and concerns at the foot of the cross.

It is only through developing a trust in the Lord that we, as overcomers, learn to experience the peace that passes all understanding throughout the storms of life. Many times, the overcomer will feel as if she is taking more steps back than forward; as if there is no progression. Over time, the overcomer will also learn that it will be okay as time after time the Lord brings her through the trial and there is no longer any reason to doubt He will do it again for the next one. I freely admit that this was an area in which I repeatedly struggled on my journey towards overcoming. At last, I learned that it was not necessary to see something in the natural in order to believe it was going to be true. I learned to rest in the Lord and His promises, increasing my trust in His word. If God says it, I know I can count on it to come to pass.

Overcomers will make a conscious decision not to fear as they put their trust in the Lord. They learn to trust that His promises are true. The Bible is filled with reminders of the Lord's trustworthiness, with reminders of generations who have gone before who have also trusted. My mind goes to the Hebrews wandering in the desert for forty years (Numbers 32, KJV), and, yes, they questioned what God was doing, but He was always with them, without a doubt. If they were able to trust God in their trials, why can't we?

Often when we've been hurt in the past—when those we've trusted let us down—trust in the present will come slowly. I encourage you to remember: those people were only human, and, as such, they were flawed by their sins. People will let you down, you will get hurt, and your trust will most likely get broken. But have heart: there is One who will never let you down. He bought you at such a great price; you can trust He will come through for you. Too many believers walk away because they lose this particular battle for their faith, quitting before they can win the battle for trust.

In the role of an overcomer, you will need to stop looking at your circumstances and firmly place your gaze upon Him. Remind yourself that He never disappoints; He is always there and is always faithful. Overcomers determine to always trust Him because of the simple fact that He has always been their God, despite what others may say. Trust Him as you realize that neither of you is going anywhere; no one is leaving anyone. Trust in those times when following Him defies all rational explanation; there are times when what He has called us to be obedient to makes no sense whatsoever but feels so very right. In such times, the best way to show our trust is to step out in faith, believing He will provide. When it came to the publishing of this book, that is exactly what I determined to do: move ahead until He stopped me. At one point, I was encouraged by my son that if the Lord wants this book published, He will provide a way—I'm trusting He will (and if you're reading this, He has!)

Eventually, the overcomer will arrive at the point of trusting Him completely, allowing Him to make all the decisions—mainly, allowing Him to be God. When you allow the Lord to be the Lord of your life, you will learn to rest in Him when the storms hit. You are learning to trust His timing as you develop both your faith and your trust. For the overcomer, running straight into His arms isn't a last resort, but rather a first choice.

For me, before I could trust Him completely, I had to come to the end of myself. One day, I looked up and realized there was something still holding me back from trusting the Lord, but I just couldn't put my finger on what it was. Eventually, I realized that it was logic that was refusing to allow me to make any progress. I mistakenly thought any promises, any words from the Lord, needed to be based in the natural before I could understand how a promise would come about. But we don't need that; we merely need faith that what He says will come to pass. It was then, in that moment, that I knew I needed to stop overthinking and allow my heart to rule in favor of trusting because the Lord was speaking to my heart, not my brain. In order to overcome, I needed to allow myself to rest as I depended on the work of God. I needed to release power and control as I submitted to His will for my life, even when—or especially when—that life did not look as expected.

The story of Abraham in Genesis 12 comes to mind. This man did not question God, but just trusted Him completely. He trusted that when God said that he and Sarah would have their promised child, regardless of age, they would! Abraham did not question his or Sarah's ability to have this child, he merely took God at His word. The Message translation provides an interpretation which perfectly sums up what the attitude should be for an overcomer. It reads: "He plunged into the promise and came up strong, ready for God, sure that God would make good on what he had said" (Romans, 4:19-25). Like Abraham, we need to plunge into our promise and make ourselves ready for what God is able to do. Your situation may appear hopeless, but with God, nothing is impossible!

Due to your status as an overcomer, you can believe that regardless of what you see with your eyes, God's got this and

He's got you. He can restore all that the enemy has stolen from you. You don't have to be afraid; you don't have to act out of desperation. Just believe that He can do the impossible. Because of the work done on the cross, the battle is won and you are already victorious. To be honest, this wasn't always how it was for me; for there was a time in my life in which the fiery trials had sucked all the oxygen from the air around me. How could I trust a God who had allowed this tragedy to strike one of His beloved? Based on the circumstances, how could I ever trust anyone again? But it was here—in the midst of the fire, gasping for breath—that I learned I could trust Him to provide for my every need. When there was no oxygen to be found in my environment as a result of the fire, He provided the air I needed in order to survive. I can trust that He will do so again if necessary, and so can you.

Just because you cannot see your promise in the natural does not mean you cannot believe what His word says or that you cannot believe in the promise that is coming. God said it, and that settles it! In addition to His every word being trustworthy and true, God's character is such that He cannot break His promises to you. Rest assured; "But truly God has listened; he has attended to the voice of my prayer" (Psalm 66:19, ESV). We can trust Him no matter what life may bring, as is written in the hymn *Simply Trusting,* by Edgar P. Stites: "Even when my faith is small, trusting Jesus, that is all".

Chapter 7

Hope Ignites

Expectations. We all have them. We dream and then eagerly await the fulfillment of those dreams. We pray and do the same as we confidently await the desired results, hoping all the while that they will come into being. Scriptures remind us, "Life motivation comes from the deep longings of the heart, and the passion to see them fulfilled urges you onward" (Proverbs 16:26, TPT).

Without hope, we are lost. Without passion—and by passion I mean that intense drive that propels you ever onward towards your dream—we all too easily lose direction, and our lives become empty and meaningless. Hope becomes the kindling that ignites the passion in our hearts, a passion which sustains us even in the most difficult of times. Maintaining hope is one of the most challenging aspects to your journey towards overcoming. Without hope, life doesn't seem worth living. Each day holds no excitement; the simple act of getting out of bed requires more effort than you can muster. Scriptures even remind us, "Hope deferred maketh the heart sick: but when the desire cometh, it is a tree of life" (Proverbs 13:12, KJV). When we live a life of hope, we greet each morning with a sense of excitement in anticipation of what that day might bring. There is also hope associated with seeing your dream come to fruition, but the longer you have to wait for that dream to come true, the more difficult it may become to keep that dream alive.

When our passions are ignited as a result of hope, even those problems which were once viewed as insurmountable have now become minor inconveniences. This enthusiasm sets our heart on fire as we follow our passions, causing us to live a fulfilled life as great things are done for the Lord. These same passions are further ignited as enjoyment in life increases and we experience abundant life while here on earth. Too many overcomers never make it to this point, giving up before pursuing their passions, abandoning their dreams because they fail to realize their breakthrough is just around the corner. But if you can hang on until that dream comes into being, the rewards are priceless.

We need to fan those flames within our hearts; I call these passions "destiny desires". You know the ones I mean: the dreams that keep you up at night, those ideas to change the world, those reasons for being. Few things in life are more beautiful than watching an individual who is following a passion. It is encouraging; we want to be like them, and we can.

In order to reach that ignition point, the coals within your heart must be rekindled; restored hope equals ignited passions. How do we flip the switch of our passions to the "on" position?

Pay attention to your dreams, to the activities that make you come most alive, to what people say you do well. What topics cause you to get up on your soapbox and preach a message to all who will listen? What makes you angry? What brings tears to your eyes? Your answer will point you in the direction of your destiny.

Sometimes circumstances of life may pull you away from your calling, but don't lose hope. The storms of life may knock you off course, nevertheless, you can trust God to bring you to an even better destination. Remain focused on Christ and believe that one day you will return to the pursuit of those dreams. Keep in mind that He would not have placed them in your heart unless He was also going to make them come to pass. We are reminded in Scriptures, "Being confident of this very thing, that he which hath begun a good work in you will perform it until the day of Jesus Christ" (Philippians 1:6, KJV).

Keeping hope alive throughout the trials of life is a challenge for even the strongest overcomer, as it is in the trials that hope is most easily snuffed out. Without hope, that fiery passion is extinguished before even being lit. When we put off hope for a later time, our todays don't seem worth living. Little joy is found in life, and we find ourselves dealing with a dangerous, depressing darkness that threatens to engulf us. Without hope, people perish. Without hope, life doesn't seem to be worth living. Without hope, we become ineffective in the work of advancing the Kingdom. All is not lost; do not lose this precious element of life, dear overcomer. Since we are believers in Christ, we have an eternal hope residing within us in the person of the Holy Spirit, and with the Holy Spirit, there is always hope, as we see in the following verse: "Now the God of hope fill you with all joy and peace in believing, that ye may abound in hope, through the power of the Holy Ghost" (Romans 15:13, KJV).

There may be moments when we are too afraid to hope due to past disappointments. As the overcomer you have become, I know you are learning to put your trust in Jesus, trusting your faith to see you through. Think for a moment on how many things we do by faith. We get into a car, believing that it will start when we turn the key. We sit in a chair, trusting that it will hold our weight and not break down just as it has done numerous times before. We trust our phone will have service and our call will go through, just like it has done in the past. But all this is nothing compared to what God can do when we place our hope in Him. There is nothing too small or too large about your life in which our mighty God is not concerned. God cares about our destiny dreams; He wants to see them fulfilled as much as we do. He wants to breathe that breath of hope upon our passions in order to keep the fire burning brightly within our hearts.

The Lord knows that hope is vital to living life abundantly. He knows that we need it to get out of bed in the morning and see us not just through the day, but through the fiery trials of life as well. If He knows this, so does the enemy. That is why the evil one works so diligently to steal our hope away, as his greatest desire is our distraction and destruction. Satan knows that if he can cause us to lose hope we will also take our eyes off of Jesus as we focus on the problem rather than the greatness of our Lord. The enemy knows that if he can destroy our passion for our destiny dreams, we will become ineffective in furthering the Kingdom. Sadly, all too often and all too easily, we fall into the trap of the enemy, dousing the flames of our passion and losing all hope.

For the overcomer, hope is essential, and keeping it can, at times, be a daily battle. For many of us, we reach a point when we must decide to persevere or give up. If this is true for you, realize that you are not alone. In fact, you are in the company of such Bible greats as Job and David: both faced great trials, both persevered, and both came through the fire shining brightly. Those who have gone before us have fought the battle between flesh and spirit; they have chosen to stand firm and their stories are shared so that you might be encouraged, just as sharing your story will encourage future overcomers.

The fiercest battle that each overcomer will eventually face is to keep their hope when circumstances would have them give up—when days, weeks, months, even years of praying result in an unchanged situation, or when it seems like God is not listening or even present. All hope-filled overcomers face multiple battles in which a decision must be made: *will I remain faithful to my Lord—particularly when life is not going smoothly—or will I give up?* In many of life's trials it will seem as if God is nowhere to be found, but the reality is that that is when He is closest to you. He hasn't left your side and He is always with you. He will never leave you or forsake you.

We can always have hope. Not in ourselves or our own actions, but in the fact that others before us have gone through the fire and come through the other side. We can pick up our Bibles and read these stories. We can find the books written by missionaries who have kept their hope in the face of great trials and persecution; books written by ordinary believers meant to encourage us on our Jesus-walk. There are numerous sources available, but the majority of this journey is personal. The decision for hope—and yes, every overcomer is required to make this choice—requires us to look beyond the circumstances directly before us as we develop a heavenly perspective towards our life. Circumstances may look hopeless in the natural, but that is a perfect opportunity to choose hope, even as it defies all logic. You need to trust that, in this moment, the Lord will make a way even then there appears to be no logical way.

By keeping hope alive, we keep those passions for our destiny dreams burning brightly as well. Overcomers maintain a determined focus on Jesus in spite of the efforts of the enemy to distract them as this hope is maintained based on His promises. Even in the face of unchanging circumstances, hope that is kept alive allows you to continue in spite of great adversity.

There may also be battles in which we have seemingly lost all hope, believing there is nothing left. It is in these times that the Holy Spirit whispers in our hearts, encouraging us to try one more time. Confrontation of personal enemies, such as your fears or your past, will allow victories that fan the flames of your passions and hope. In these skirmishes, don't focus overly much on your weaknesses because it is here that God steps in to complete you; those weak areas just might be used to ignite the passion in another's life.

As an overcomer experiencing these victories, your life will be flooded with joy and confident expectation. Igniting your passion will reveal your purpose and destiny, the very reason for which you've been born, and through it all you will also be expanding the Kingdom. But in order to achieve this ignition, you are going to need to develop a breakthrough mentality as you learn to tear down those mental barriers.

Part of that breakthrough mentality consists of knowing that you have something unique to offer; however, before you can offer hope to another, you need to know what you bring. Knowing who we are in Christ enables us to help others discover who they are. If I truly believe I am the daughter of the King, I will conduct myself differently and walk into overwhelming situations with the greatest confidence. Overcomers become testimonies of what God can do, ultimately becoming living advertisements for Jesus. Allowing Christ to work through you will cause people to notice something different about you. They will be drawn to you, and you will become contagious in your faith.

Throughout your fiery trials, you will notice a new fire that has been ignited within your heart by the Holy Spirit. I can truthfully say that as the Lord tried my heart, He was turning it into something that He could use. The knowledge gained as a result of the fire was too valuable to remain hidden, burning too brightly as it spilled over into a passion that would help others discover who they are in Christ. You will find yourself wanting to encourage others so that they may then be drawn to Him. Scriptures state, "And then go and tell the coming generation of the care and compassion of our God" (Psalm 48:13, TPT).

There is so much pain associated with the fire, but there is no other way. Stand firm, overcomer; it is a way worth every tear and every heartache as you step into your reason for being on this earth. The pit, the trials, the fire—these are all times of refining, polishing, and preparing for your destiny. Use these trials wisely because, as we overcome, the trials come to be more about the process than the end result. They are about who you are becoming and what you are learning along the way.

On this journey to overcoming you also experience a satisfaction that resonates deep within your soul as you discover your life's purpose. Your trials have prepared you for your Esther moment; they have prepared you for such a time as this. As a result of your hardships, you can better understand the trials of others. Many times, we don't understand what another is going through until we experience it for ourselves. The fire and trials allow you to better comfort another from your new position of greater understanding.

When all you can see is darkness, hope illuminates the road by providing the spark needed to ignite your hope. This in turn ignites your passion to continue on in the pursuit of your destiny dream. You need this hope to get you through the rough times, to pull you out of the pit of despair, and to keep you moving forward. The surest place to put your hope in is God, as He is sure and steadfast, proving to be our certainty in an uncertain world. Hope in the Lord is firm and secure as it anchors our soul (Hebrews 6:19, KJV).

With hope, nothing can extinguish your passion!

Chapter 8

All that I've Lost, I've Found Again in Jesus

Throughout life, the storms will toss us about on the waves, and while this causes turmoil for a season, it needn't be true for a lifetime as there is One who can firmly anchor us. These storms often bring us to a crisis in our faith; it is here that you will need to decide, once and for all, who He is for you. You may be called upon to relinquish a lot, but you may also find all you need in Christ.

It's all about Jesus. Read that again if you need to: it's all about Him. Our flesh bristles at that statement, doesn't it, as it chimes in with "What about me?" In the grand scheme of things, it *isn't* about us, and it *is* about Him. The sooner we realize that fact, the sooner life becomes easier; the sooner we compare what we are giving up to what we are gaining, the sooner we realize we aren't giving up anything we can't live without.

Scripture describes what I was feeling perfectly: "The sorrows of death compassed me, and the floods of ungodly men made me afraid. The sorrows of hell compassed me about, the snares of death prevented me" (Psalm 18:4-5, KJV). It truly felt as if death would be preferable to what I had been enduring; my life had become a living hell as trial after trial buffeted me and the enemy attempted to break me. There will be times in your Jesus-walk when the enemy will throw everything he has at you in an attempt to destroy you. The choice is yours: a step closer to the Lord or a step away from Him. When you make the right choice—the choice to draw closer to the Lord—you lose little in comparison to what you gain.

Even now, years after my crisis, I still struggle with the losses. There are still days when all I can see is how much I've had to give up, focusing only on the negative. Too often we concentrate on what we have given up to follow Jesus while forgetting to pay attention to what we have gained. Pause for a moment to reflect: what would you give in exchange for your soul? What is more valuable, your comfort or your spiritual growth? I freely admit the transformation will not be easy, but with great sacrifice will come great reward.

My experience in getting from there to here has been filled with many tears, breakdowns, and meltdowns, as it has undoubtedly been for you as well, my dear overcomer. First the old must be demolished before the rebuilding can begin. That which doesn't point you to Christ must be stripped away. Much of our past life can be released. Those negative, useless behaviors and possessions will be easy to let go of, but what about those parts of life which we aren't so eager to be rid of? Some behaviors, because of their familiarity, will be more difficult to release. However, looking back, you may find yourself wishing you would have let them go earlier, so that you could have gained the valuable wisdom that came from doing so much sooner.

Many times we think that we know best: think we know what we need best, or think we know the best direction our lives should take when what we really need to do is trust that the Lord knows best. Honestly, we don't have a clue, even though we fool ourselves into thinking we do. As we continue on our journey towards letting Jesus be all we need, we must trust Him to supply exactly what we need at the exact moment we need it. Much of what He provides we will eagerly accept, but there will be some changes that we question. Let's be honest: for most of us, change is uncomfortable, as the majority of us prefer the familiar over the unknown. But, why settle for crumbs when God is about to rain manna from heaven upon you? We are reminded in Scriptures, "Not that I speak in respect of want: for I have learned, in whatsoever state I am, therewith to be content" (Philippians 4:11, KJV). Trust that as God removes, He will replace; what replaces the old will not just be better, but the best. Be content with what He is doing in your life as He helps you find His Son, Jesus.

Think for a moment how much of life actually pulls us away from a relationship with Jesus. Even good, wholesome activities can take us from our first love, Christ Jesus, because anything that we put before God becomes an idol in our life. It may feel as if you are losing or have lost everything when the trials hit, but you are actually discovering what it is you need. You are discovering that all you truly need is Jesus. On particularly good days, I can see that all I've given up has been worth it, but there are still days when the enemy sneaks in and fills my mind with his lies. I imagine the same has happened to you. The enemy, as the liar he is, shouts false accusations that you've given up your life for nothing as he questions where God is in all of this mess. We need to be on guard against this, ever ready to repel these attacks. There is nothing you can do, nothing you can own that will define you; your identity is found in Christ and Christ alone.

You may find yourself longing for what has been lost or taken from you; I suggest you examine those thoughts in order to determine what it is you are truly yearning for. It may not be your former life you are craving, but rather those feelings of belonging, security, or even identity, as defined by marriage or employment. Take a moment as you realize that your identity is found only in Christ and is not based on performance or possession. I urge you to realize what it is that you have found; take a step closer to Him. You will realize that what you are gaining as a result of these trials is a life-giving relationship with your Heavenly Father. In Him, we come alive and are found. In Him, we are sons and daughters of the most High God. In Him, we are heirs to all that His Kingdom holds. In Him, we discover that we are royalty in possession of resurrection power; dearly loved, sheltered, and protected.

As you take this step towards Christ and overcoming, you will realize that it is a daily choice to follow Jesus—a daily choice to willingly sacrifice your life and desires in order to give precedence to His. Faith must be put on daily as a conscious choice to look to Jesus when the world paints a different picture. As you make this choice, you will also discover how the Lord replaces your good with His best. Slowly, over time, numerous trials, copious tears, and hard work, you will find your attitude shifting as you voluntarily submit to His will; releasing all that is unnecessary as you become broken before God. Let go of those expectations and that self-limiting behavior as you journey towards Christ. Abandon those notions and beliefs that do not align with His. In doing so, you will gain more than you ever could imagine as Jesus becomes real to you because, as you discard that which is no longer useful, your understanding of who He for you will change. As your desires align with God's, so much of what you think you need holds no true purpose. He is all you need. All that you lose, you will find again in Jesus.

Jesus becomes real as He proves His steadfastness over and over. Scripture will become real as you find Jesus; as real as if written specifically for your life. Your relationship with your Heavenly Father, along with your faith, will flourish. The Bible will become filled with truth that applies to you and your situation, truth that you could not receive in the past, but, once you find Jesus, you are now able to take it all in.

On this journey to finding what you've lost in Jesus, many days may find you wishing life could have taken a different turn; wishing you could have avoided all this pain. But, dear one, there are times in life when the pain brings revelation, when the fire brings beauty from the ashes left behind. Psalm 23 speaks not just of death, but also of being in such a state that death is actually preferred when circumstances threaten to overwhelm.

Remember, He is with you in the fire and the flood as well as on the mountaintop.

On this journey, you've learned to leave the decision making up to Him, completely trusting His judgement over your own. You've learned to trust that, when you ask, He will provide. Jobs, relationships, your future—everything can be placed in His more than capable hands. Scripture reminds us "This one thing I know-God is on my side!" (Psalm, 56:9, TPT). There is no need for anxiety or fear; there is no place for them in a relationship with the Lord.

One of the most basic human needs is acceptance; it is through a relationship with Jesus that this longing within your soul can be filled. This wound is often present in many of our lives, often festering for lack of treatment or attention. An injury, when left unattended, isn't able to heal, and will often affect our behavior. How many of us attempt to heal these wounds through continued harmful behavior, like an addict who needs more and more of their addiction to get another high? There is only One who can bring healing; as you discover your true identity in Jesus, He brings the restorative salve that will heal all wounds.

Knowing to whom you belong allows you to experience the storms of life with a completely different approach: that of peace. As the storms rage about you, you will come to recognize and anticipate experiencing the peace that passes all understanding. As you meditate on the promises as found in His word, you will recognize that you haven't lost a thing. In fact, you've found what you have been seeking all along. You will come to understand the things you initially thought you couldn't live without are no longer necessary for your life with Christ as contentment has become a way of life, regardless of circumstances. Losses have been accepted as they have prepared the overcomer for this time, and place in life. Gratitude and appreciation are present daily.

For me personally on my journey to overcoming, I walked through a season in which the trials threatened to overwhelm me. The depressing darkness of this season found me struggling with my faith, often filling my prayers with the request of *Lord, don't let me give up on you.* Thankfully, He didn't let me down. Even in those darkest of moments, somehow I knew He would never give up on me; in fact, that knowledge is what kept me going. Over time, as the trials persisted, I continued to turn to Him with increased frequency. It was in this darkest time that I experienced the greatest increase in my love towards Christ. I wish that I could tell you this was an easy, overnight transformation, but it was anything but. It was here that I learned to look to Him as I found peace, rather than being overwhelmed by my circumstances. Maybe in those times when you feel as if you are breaking, you are actually being strengthened, as you honestly, openly admit you can't go on. It is then that He carries you.

Through this entire season of being tried, my faith has been strengthened. Faith allows me to know I will see God's goodness, turns my heart completely towards Him, and assures me that I am all He says I am as it reminds me that I now belong to Him, my God and My king. As the daughter of the King, I now know that I am royalty as I walk into any situation in the natural with that truth firmly shielding me.

Because I've learned that all I need is Jesus, I have been transformed from a woman who barely believed she was loved by the Father into a woman whose heart now spills over with love from her Heavenly Father. I've also become a woman eager to share the message of His transforming love with others. I was an orphan, merely waiting to be taught how to accept the love of my Heavenly Father so that I might blossom into who I was created to be. Now that I know to whom I belong, I can rest securely in His love. I no longer need to work so diligently to hide all my flaws as He knows me completely and loves me still—loves me even more because of them. Even though He allowed me to experience the fire, including the pain of the flames, He protected me the entire time I was in the midst of it. There can no longer be any doubt that I belong to Him.

In reality, what I have I lost? A lot of junk I really didn't need. That heavy baggage from my past filled with shame, guilt, anger, and inadequacy that had been preventing me from forward movement has been left behind. Normally, losing luggage is not a good thing, but in this case it is. My lost luggage contained all those things that were holding me back; now, I've repacked my bags with what I've gained in Jesus: self-respect, confidence, and purpose. While I was losing my baggage from my past, I found what I needed; Jesus Christ. I found out He was real and that He was for me. So now when I look back, I realize what I lost actually had very little significance, possessing only the value that I had placed—or rather misplaced—upon it, whereas all that I have gained is priceless.

As more and more of me was burned away in the fiery trials, I realized all that really mattered was Jesus. For too many years I was distracted with the differing views over baptism—should it be sprinkling or immersion?—or music—was it permissible to listen to contemporary praise and worship music, or was it required that I stick to traditional hymns? But one day I realized none of that truly matters. All that matters is a saving knowledge of Christ. Once you remove yourself from the arguments surrounding faith, you are then free to love others as the Father would have you love them. We don't need to get caught up in all those frivolous debates that can cause a church to split. It's all about loving God with all your heart, soul, and mind. It's all about you, Jesus. That's the beautiful simplicity of the Gospel.

At one point, I experienced a dream in which everything was whirling about as if in a tornado scene from an old black and white movie. The objects in my dream were blurry as they swirled about my peripheral vision, but for some reason the very center of my field of vision was completely clear. There was someone in this focal point, and, without being able to provide a description of the individual, I knew it was Jesus. It was here, in the very center—in my very center—that I experienced a clear view of Christ. That's when I knew: He really is all you need. He really can bring you peace in the storm.

All that I've lost, I've found again in Jesus. Allow me to share a few words that I've written along my journey; on the evening these sentiments were initially written, my thoughts had turned to how far I had come in my Jesus-walk.

This is on my heart tonight: I am a world changer...an atmosphere shifter...a survivor and a thriver! I am royalty. And it is huge that I can stand before you and say that. Because I am also a victim of domestic violence and struggle with both worth and value. I have experienced homelessness, joblessness, the humiliation of public assistance, rejection of friends, church, and family...along with many more trials.... I would cry on my way to work, while getting ready for work, while driving home from work...and even occasionally at work. Some Fridays, I would go home after work and never leave the house until Monday morning when it was time to go to work again. There were meltdowns, breakdowns....and any other tragedy one might think of. My prayer was continually "Lord, don't let me give up on you". And He didn't let me down. Somehow I knew He would never give up on me...and that's what kept me going. As the trials increased, strengthened and continued—I continued to turn to Him. He became my rock...my fortress...my protector...my Father...my everything. I learned to turn to Him for every need...physical and spiritual. Crying out for Him to fill the longing in my soul...to fill the emptiness that can only be filled by Him. Now, my continual prayer has become"...Jesus, I love you...I love you...I love you! Fill me with more of your Holy Spirit. Don't relent until you have my all". And again, He does not disappoint. It is a time of stepping into my destiny...a time of great restoration of ALL that the locust have eaten...of all that has been stolen from me. But that doesn't mean I can rest, yet. I'm coming to find that being close to the finish line means one last, great battle...the battle for my destiny. I can't rest yet...I'm not yet home. But this battle is fought on my knees...claiming every verse that I now KNOW to be true and applicable to me.

Chains have been broken...lies replaced with truths...Because with FAITH...I know I will see God's goodness...with FAITH, my heart has turned completely towards Him...with FAITH, I know I am ALL He says I am...and He says I am His own! I am the daughter of the King...I am royalty and I walk into my destiny believing that truth! I walk into the world and the sweet presence of the Holy Spirit draws others to the Father through me. People are drawn to me...they share their story with me...and I lead them to the Father.

Just as you, my dear overcomer, will do.

Chapter 9

Unexpected Beauty from Ashes

From the cocoon emerges the beautiful butterfly; from the oyster comes the lovely pearl; from the fire comes the purest gold. Beauty can be found in the most unexpected places, including among the smoldering ashes of the fire. Many of us face seasons in life that look nothing like we expected; this is not an easy place to find yourself. Perhaps your marriage failed, you were unexpectedly let go from the job you thought you'd retire from, a loved one was surprisingly taken from this life much too soon—the list is endless. Whatever it is that you face, keep in mind that God wants to change your life; He wants to make it better because He loves you too much to allow you to remain as you are. As a result of walking through the flames, you become more beautiful as you are transformed into His image.

I had led a relatively quiet, peaceful life as a believer in Christ for years until the trials hit. Oh, don't get me wrong, raising (and homeschooling) two children had its challenges, as did juggling the swing shift my then-husband worked, but, overall, since I had accepted Jesus as my Savior, my life had been undisturbed and uninterrupted.

Until one day it wasn't. In the blink of an eye, my life as I knew it was gone, and by my choosing. I had to walk away from the life I thought that I had been building as the situation in my house reached an ignition point that, once lit, would become inextinguishable. In three days, my children and I made difficult decisions as to what to take and what to leave behind; we couldn't take everything we wanted, or even what we needed. We left so much of our life behind: dreams, pets, possessions; our support system and financial resources; even our home as we endured a brief period of homelessness. I was not prepared for this and I was scared beyond anything I had ever experienced, but I needed to be strong for my children even though all I really wanted was for someone to tell me things would be okay.

In this particular fire, I walked through public assistance, a never-ending job hunt, court dates for custody and support, two broken elbows (on two separate occasions), financial hits, loss of transportation (twice), and more as life continued on. Children who once had been homeschooled still needed an education and now needed to attend a brick-and-mortar school. I was reminded that life continues even in the fire as these same children went on to graduate high school, attend college, and even graduate from college. What was I doing during this time? Job hunting and completing degrees of my own as I pursued first a bachelor's and then a master's degree.

But all of this fire-walking had a purpose: to prepare me for my next assignment. Let me encourage you on your fire-walking journey: walking through the fire prepares you for your destiny and, as painful as it may be, is necessary for advancement. Even while dream after dream was sacrificed for mere survival, a new dream was being birthed from the ashes of this season. All along, I knew that one day I would take this debilitating pain and use it to help other women in similar circumstances. As an added bonus—the greatest bonus—my relationship with the Lord was forever altered, as was I.

God took these attacks meant for my destruction and turned them into something meant for my good as I walked through the fire. While He molded me into a closer image of Himself, I also became a living advertisement of what He can do in a person's life. The enemy often tempted me with his lies as he whispered suggestions into my ear, hinting that the pain would stop if I turned my back on the Lord. I certainly wanted the trials to stop, so quitting was quite a temptation. I still remember moments when I would beg the Lord *not* to let me walk away from Him. Thankfully, He did draw me closer—and then closer still!

But it is here in the fire that our most difficult decisions must be made; we must choose to live by what God is saying in His word, even though—or particularly when—the expected result is nowhere in sight. The road may present a challenging uphill climb, but, trust me, beauty can be found all along the way, not just at the summit. Stand firm in the belief that your prayers are both heard and will be answered; after all, that's faith!

When we initially find ourselves facing a life that looks nothing like we had expected, disappointment and anger find their way into our attitude. In order to successfully get through this season, overcomers need to face the harmful emotions from their past and send them packing! Unfortunately, life isn't fair and bad things will happen to good people. Let's not forget about the ever-present effects of sin as well, as sin has taken a world perfectly created by God and tarnished it. We read in Scriptures, "Wherefore, as by one man sin entered into the world, and death by sin; and so death passed upon all men, for that all have sinned" (Romans 5:12, KJV). Simply put, we are all guilty of sinning, and, while this is inarguably true, there is also a solution for this problem of sin which is found in Jesus, as we read in the following verse: "But thanks be to God, which giveth us the victory through our Lord Jesus Christ" (1 Corinthians 15:57, KJV). It is through Christ that lives are transformed and sin is dealt with once and for all.

As we sift through the ashes of our life, care must be taken to discover and extinguish any glowing embers of bitterness. Accompanying any unexpected turn in life is soul-crushing disappointment, a disappointment which must be faced before beauty can be found. Since we are believers in Christ, we often mistakenly believe that He will keep us from all harm, and He will, in His own way, but His way might not always be the way we want. For too many working towards overcoming, the misguided belief that no evil will touch our lives hinders our spiritual growth. We forget that God allows these trials to enter our lives so that we are able to achieve greater maturity. We read in Scriptures, "Knowing this, that the trying of your faith worketh patience. But let patience have her perfect work, that ye may be perfect and entire, wanting nothing" (James 1:3-4, KJV).

We have to remember that most of life is about the journey and what's been learned along the way rather than "arriving". We learn that these same trials which threaten to destroy actually can be used for our benefit as we release control of our lives into His more than capable hands. You will come to the understanding that the Lord knows what you need better than you do. Many of His "no's" may actually keep you from harm. As you relinquish control to Him, you will develop your ability to remain flexible towards His plans for your life. Old expectations are released in order to welcome the new. Hope based on His promises begins to develop, and, as a result, joy and contentment increase. Much like Paul and Silas in prison, you may even find yourself singing songs of praise to the Lord in the midst of life's hardships (Acts 16:16-40). For the overcomer, the ability to rise above this disappointment and bitterness will most likely not happen overnight. By remaining focused on Him and trusting that His way is the best way, overcomers will learn that life doesn't look as expected and that is perfectly acceptable. In fact, it could become more beautiful than ever imagined!

Beauty from ashes comes in when God takes the mess that your life has become as a result of all these trials and turns it into something amazing. Just because your life didn't turn out as expected doesn't mean that it can't still be amazing, or that you can no longer serve God. Scriptures remind us: "To appoint unto them that mourn in Zion, to give unto them beauty for ashes, the oil of joy for mourning, the garment of praise for the spirit of heaviness; that they might be called trees of righteousness, the planting of the Lord, that he might be glorified" (Isaiah 61:3, KJV). The fire isn't something that only destroys; it also can create beauty. The original purpose of the fire, as designed by the enemy, is our destruction. God can take the fire started by the enemy and make it a different type of fire: the one ignited within your heart.

I understand that it may still be difficult for you to realize that there can be beauty birthed from the ashes. After all, how can God use your crushed expectations to bring about good? How can good come from divorce, death, or destruction?

Eventually the overcomer accepts that nothing in life will ever be the same again; there will be no return to the former, comfortable ways of living. There is only one direction to go: forward, ho! You must decide if you will remain as is, wallowing in self-pity over your losses, or choose option number two, blazing a new trail. This new trail is unpaved and contains no markings, but, by taking it, you create a new road for the generations that will travel it after you. It is never an easy choice, but it is a rewarding one, as blazing these new trails also brings new territory for the Kingdom.

As the Father trains you to seek this beauty resulting from destruction, He also changes your definition of beauty. For the pre-overcomer, beauty had been based on outward appearances and perfection. For the individual new to overcoming, beauty is found in the scars that have resulted from the burns of their walk through the fire. Wear your scars proudly, because they tell the story of what you have achieved.

When the fire initially begins, you, as a budding overcomer, may have no idea how the Lord will take what appears to be failure after failure and turn it into a thing of beauty. The discovery that an amazing message to the world will come from your life's greatest mess is a result of more time spent in the refining fire. You learn that He will use your time in the fire to draw you closer to Him, molding you into His image. Now that's a thing of beauty!

One key component to discovering the beauty buried deeply within your ashes is keeping an open mind and heart before the Lord as you accept the possibilities of a grand future designed by the Creator of the universe. At times, as the pain becomes too much and as the fire burns too brightly, this concept is incomprehensible and the overcomer may still view themselves as unworthy. Ever so slowly, the fire will allow you to release control of your life to Him as your story intertwines with His design for your life. He becomes your center as His light guides you along the smoke filled road before you.

The fire, along with the refining process, burns away all that is no longer necessary leaving behind pure gold. You, as the beautiful overcomer that you are, have been purged and refined until only the purest form of gold remains. The season in the fire may have been a long one, but now you have your beautiful ending as you learn the fire can do more good than harm. As you progress, your heart begins to take hold of the tiniest glimmer of hope that sparkling gold will begin to peak through the dusty ashes, a hope that continues to form until it becomes a thing of marvelous beauty.

Exactly what does this beauty that I continually refer to look like? It looks like Jesus, and it results in the purest of gold as the cleansing fire produces a beauty that outshines any other, reflecting Him. The burning away of the dross removes all of those things about you that were not part of your new creation in Him. The lies? Up in smoke. The doubt, shame, and fear? Burst into flames. Unworthiness? Poof, it is gone! In the fire, overcomers are polished and refined. This is not the quick, painless process towards becoming shiny and new we all hope it to be. Scriptures remind us, "Therefore if any man be in Christ, he is a new creature: old things are passed away; behold, all things are become new" (2 Corinthians 5:17, KJV), but we frequently forget the discomfort this becoming may entail. There will likely be numerous occasions when you want to quit, but don't! Stand firm; it will be worth it all.

Think how children remove a Band-Aid: slowly, hesitantly pulling it away from their skin as they try to experience as little discomfort as possible, but those attempts to avoid pain rarely succeed. The season in the fire is painful, and, in reality, the process of this refinement is much more like the debridement of a wound as a result of being burned by the fire. There can be no hesitancy as the wound requires vigorous scrubbing in order to remove the decaying flesh. This flesh, if left untreated, would eventually result in death. This flesh may require time to heal, and it may result in scars, but these same scars will one day remind you of how far the Lord has brought you on your faith-walk.

As an overcomer, you have come over the destruction meant by the fiery trials; you have come over what the enemy meant for harm. As a result, your life is now pregnant with the possibilities that have been stirred up from within the ashes. It is here, in our lowest state, where we find our Savior. In the fiery pit of despair, we find Jesus. He and He alone can comfort us in our most painful moments; He and He alone is the salve required for the healing of the burns from the fire. It is here, in the midst of the smoking ashes, that we realize our greatest need for Him. Much like a forest fire, the ashes left behind are used to fertilize the new growth that comes after the fire dies down. This fertilizer nourishes the soil, providing the seedling—you—with the necessary nourishment for growth; you need the fertilizer supplied by the ashes of these fiery trials for your season of beautiful growth.

There is another characteristic of fire that we have yet to discuss: the smoke. The smoke often comes from the enemy in an attempt to distract the overcomer from realizing their potential. Eventually, this smoke will dissipate, revealing that all is not as it initially seemed. Too often, overcomers adopt a mindset in which every mistake, regardless of size, is viewed as being the end of the world. I can assure you that it is not. This mindset may darken your world as it fills it with smoke and your tear-filled eyes prohibit you from seeing clearly. As this smoke is blown away by the winds of truth, you discover that the fire is not the cataclysmic event you originally thought it to be.

Dear overcomers, you might be experiencing the cleansing fire right now. Realize this: it won't last forever, but it does require time for the embers to cool. In due course, the flames will die down, but, more importantly, remember that you aren't in the fire alone. He is right by your side. The time spent in the fire allows the Lord to perfect you, ultimately resulting in your being refined and polished, shining brightly for Jesus.

By now, in the fading glow left by the fire, your concept of beauty is being redefined. As the smoke dissipates in the breeze, the faulty beliefs of beauty also disappear and are replaced with a definition set forth by the Lord. He has added scars to the list of what He calls beautiful, along with all of your unique imperfections. As a result of a relationship with Him, much like Moses' glowing countenance when he returned from time spent with the Lord (Exodus 34:35, KJV), your face shines with the glory of the Lord. Now, when you, as an overcomer, have occasion to give your testimony—bragging on what the Lord has done—your very countenance changes; eyes sparkle, face glows, smile widens—now that's beautiful!

My dear overcomer, you will make it through the fire. There will be many times when you just want it all to end, and it will, eventually. Until then, learn to rely more on Him. Seek Him. Become more like Him. Trust Him as He adjusts the bellows, increasing the heat for a moment as He burns away more of the dross. Let go of what is no longer needed. The process may include pain and trials as you walk through the hot coals of growth, but, as one who has gone through the fire before you, I can tell you that the journey through the flames will be worth it.

Your attitude will change, as will your heart, revealing more of Him in the process. Rarely would any of us choose the trials we walk through, but each trial is indispensable to the formation of you as a beautiful overcomer, transforming you into someone who resembles Christ in a greater manner. There is no other way to get to this point; it is challenging but well worth it. These trials are truly for your edification; what you think you've lost has actually been regained in Jesus as God has simultaneously broken and rebuilt you, much like bones can require re-breaking in order to be properly set. These fiery trials are God's plan to prepare you to shine through to a broken world. You've been through the fire so that you might encourage others; the fire has increased your understanding and compassion towards your fellow travelers. Once you've been in the flames, you have to help others; there is no alternate choice. You get it, you understand, and as a result you reach out, providing a bucket of hope for someone else still in the heat of the trial.

There is gold to be found in both the valley and the mountaintop; good can, and will, come from the bad in your life. Trials can bring blessings; you just need to trust the process as you look past the present to your future. So start digging—let's unearth some gold!

"O Lord, we have passed through your fire; like precious metal made pure, you've proved us, perfected us, and made us holy" (Psalm 66:10, TPT).

Mental Prisons

B etween God's love towards us and the blood of Christ, there is no chain in our lives that cannot be broken, no prison from which we cannot be released. Yet we continue to view these restraints as possessing more strength than they actually do. One of the results of experiencing the beauty hidden within the ashes is the accompanying realization that we have been locking ourselves into mental prisons. Let's engage in a reality check together: who is the true enemy that holds you back? Please don't get me wrong, there is an enemy whose main purpose is to destroy and distract, but if we really examine our lives, aren't we our own worst enemy?

See if you recognize yourself as engaging in the following behavior: each time you make a mistake or perform less than perfectly, the voice in your head begins the same old conversation, reminding you what a failure you have been, currently are, and always will be. Most likely there have been numerous individuals in your life who have chosen to speak words of death rather than life over you, but if you are completely honest, which voice is the loudest? It is what we say in the quiet of our own minds that forms the strongest locks on our mental prisons.

Our own voice is more damaging than any heard by our physical ears. It is this inner dialogue that builds the strongest chains as it continually reminds us of our failures and that we are not good enough, smart enough, or *whatever* enough. It is your own voice confining you with self-imposed restrictions as it fashions a psychological penitentiary in which your dreams and destinies have been given a life sentence. Sadly, too many overcomers have incarcerated themselves in these mental prisons with no hope for parole.

Passing such harsh sentences upon ourselves causes a lapse in memory, with one small detail often being forgotten: who holds the key that will unlock the cell. If we take a moment and examine these cells in which we have caged ourselves, we soon discover they are no more than an illusion, and prove much easier to break out of than we originally thought. Too often, we mistakenly believe that the chains that enslave us are made of the strongest iron known to man, only to discover upon closer inspection that they are actually made of the most delicate gold, therefore being easily broken. Despite this, too many of us remain chained within these mental prisons longer than necessary because we fail to make use of the resurrection power residing within us. The very same power that raised Jesus from the dead, healed the blind man, and stilled the storm dwells within us today. We are reminded: "But if the Spirit of him that raised up Jesus from the dead dwell in you, he that raised up

Christ from the dead shall also quicken your mortal bodies by his Spirit that dwelleth in you" (Romans 8:11, KJV).

How many of us remain in a prison of our own making, each bar manufactured with every "can't", "shouldn't", and "you're not good enough"? How many of us hold ourselves back by falsely believing that success will never be ours, or that we cannot be worthy of God's love? What about those of us who remain imprisoned because the lock of people pleasing is firmly in place, forgetting there is only One we should be seeking approval from? Too often we give our key of liberating power away; often, we forget we even possess this key as we also fail to make use of the breakout power of the Holy Spirit within us just waiting to be used.

In reality, a prison break could occur at any moment as the chains and locks cannot truly contain us. Had the prisoner only known her freedom has already been purchased by Christ on the cross, no prison could have held her. The key is already within her reach, she need only make use of it. Don't stay locked up one more moment! Realize you already have the power—and the key—to fling that door wide open!

In my personal journey to overcoming, I slowly learned that I had been my own warden. I had been holding the key to my freedom but had just chosen not to make use of it. I imprisoned myself for much of my life as I allowed my self-image to be based on the world's definition of me rather than the Lord's. I had sentenced myself to years of unnecessary imprisonment as I saw myself as being *less than* or *not enough.* I allowed these faulty perceptions of me to hold me back. But, the entire time, my mind was only doing what I was telling it to do: constructing a prison. As I told myself I wasn't enough, this flawed self-image controlled my actions and performance, making it nearly impossible to rise above the version I held of myself within my own mind, building those prison walls higher and higher, and all-too-effectively locking me away, prohibiting me from living life.

The strongest bars of my mental prison were built on the false beliefs of my value; I—incorrectly—believed I was not worth my Heavenly Father's love. Oh, I received salvation, but I didn't or couldn't experience His love beyond that. This flawed thinking contributed to a lie I believed that if others didn't love me, I must not be worth loving. I never realized that my worth and identity came from a Heavenly source. Looking back, I have to question if I would offer that same advice to a friend. The answer is no. If I wouldn't say something like that to a friend, why would I say it to myself? Why not treat yourself as a friend and start to tell yourself the truth: you are loved, you are valued, and you belong to the Lord.

That was only one bar of my prison; there were many more and I imagine you have a few of your own that are quite different from mine. Each one of these bars is formed by the lies we believe, the defective logic we allow to rule our lives, and any messages we've allowed through from the enemy. Did you know that the enemy is afraid of you as an overcomer? Afraid of what you might do? That is why he attacks and continually wages war against you; he is terrified by the thought of what you could do for the Kingdom if you were set free from your prison.

Think with me for a moment: how many dreams do you think go unrealized because the individual remains imprisoned? How many books go unwritten? Sermons unpreached? Prisons keep us from pursuing our destiny dreams, while breaking out allows us to freely follow our hearts. The enemy is doing a great job of helping us build those prisons, but let's do something about that. Let's stage a breakout!

All it takes is a simple shift in our thinking. By shifting our thinking, we can break out of these mental prisons and break into our destiny dreams. By shifting our thinking, we can finally be free to overcome all previous confinements. All too often, we become what we focus on. As we focus on the negative, the direction of our life follows. When we shift our focus to that which is pure, lovely, and virtuous, our life will follow that direction.

For you, as an overcomer, this shift in thinking will provide you with the key needed to unlock any and all locks found within your prison. A couple of the keys of truth on your liberating keychain may include: you are not a failure, even though you sometimes fail; while you may disappoint, you are not a disappointment; and so on. Can you see how that subtle shift in thinking changes everything? The enemy would have you view all that you do through the lens of negativity, but the Lord would have you believe the truth about you; a truth that will set you free. Just like we ought to focus on the sin rather than the sinner, we must focus on the behavior, not the person.

The overcomer must shift the thought from what they do to who they are—as well as to whom they belong. Scriptures provide numerous descriptions as to who we are in Christ. For example, "we are a chosen generation, a royal priesthood" (I Peter 2:9, KJV); "we are his workmanship" (Ephesians 2:10, KJV); once we belong to Jesus we are no longer condemned (Romans 8:1, KJV); and lastly, we become the "sons of God" (John 1:12, KJV), and, as such, heirs to everything that belongs to the Father.

An additional tool for breaking out of our mental prison is to deal with our self-image as we often allow this self-imposed limitation to hinder our walk with Jesus. In order to find this freedom all overcomers eventually reach the point of *enough*: enough of being locked up, enough of being a victim, enough of whatever it is that falsely imprisons you. When the overcomer learns to say *enough,* the authority of Christ—which has resided within them since the day of salvation—is being used as God intended. At this point, the overcomer is on their way to losing their inmate status and well on their way towards an early parole.

Remember all those lies that had formed the bars of your mental prison? Well, in order for you to be released from that prison, the lies must be dispelled. For many, the key that will unlock the door of the prison will take on a variety of forms. Here are a few that will assist you in your break out: in Song of Songs the Lord refers to us as His *beloved*; in the New Testament, we are called a new creation (2 Corinthians 5:17, KJV); learn to think of yourself as children of God (I John 1:22,

KJV); and, finally, realize that you are His friend (John 15:15, KJV). There are numerous references in the Bible describing how God sees you; it would be a great idea for you to sit down one day and do a search of your own—I'd love to hear what you come up with. As you discover how God sees you, you will experience freedom. I urge you to memorize the passages that speak to you, claim them as your own, and apply them to your life. God's promises release the shackles that had been keeping you hostage. God's Word can act as a lock pick; flinging your prison door wide open as your relationship with the Lord is strengthened.

This same shift in thinking—this focus on the positive along with God's promises—must also be applied to poor decisions of your past, as well as any incorrect beliefs. Guilt has no place outside of the prison doors. Follow the steps outlined in the following Scripture: "If we confess our sins, he is faithful and just to forgive us *our* sins, and to cleanse us from all unrighteousness" (1 John 1:9, KJV). Confess your sins, ask for forgiveness, accept it, and move forward! Don't waste another moment reminding yourself of all those poor decisions; instead, learn from them as you come to understand how all those life experiences have made you into the person you are today. Refuse to allow poor choices to imprison you any longer. Keep in mind that everything life has brought you through—the good, the bad, and the ugly—has made you into the wonderfully unique individual you currently are.

Refuse to allow these prison bars to influence your concept of self any longer! Refuse to give them the power to confine you for another moment. Consider the source of these lies: the evil one himself attempts to imprison you in order to make you ineffective for the Lord. Why allow this false imprisonment to continue for one more second? Now, there may be times when these bars are removed individually; that's okay! Stick with it, stand firm, and eventually you will be free. Keep in mind: it isn't always about the destination, but the transformation that occurs during the journey.

One final note of caution: much like the inmate who has been imprisoned so long that she cannot live in the real world, you may also experience a desire to remain in your prison. It might be all you know, and you may feel safe there. But Jesus has already overcome every power of darkness—why do we remain enslaved? Many of us say we want to change but never follow our words with action—could it be that perhaps we don't really want to change? The majority of us long to be free, long to experience the self-imposed restrictions continuing to confine us, but, for some reason unbeknownst to us, we remain firmly planted within those confining bars. Perhaps it is the familiarity of our prisons which keeps us living in them as we have been residents for years. We might not like our cell, but it's all we know and we've grown to feel comfortable in our confinement. As we've lived there, we've trained our mind to believe those lies as told to us by the enemy; further allowing him to strengthen the illusion of the lock on the cell.

Remember that key? For the overcomer, the key is found in Christ's redemptive work done on the cross. Scriptures exhort us to "Stand fast therefore in the liberty wherewith Christ hath made us free, and be not entangled again with the yoke of bondage" (Galatians 5:1, KJV). Once we have been freed by Christ, the door will be unlocked and the overcomer will experience freedom as those bars once formed by lies are removed. Finally, the inner voices are silenced. No longer can they tell you "no, you can't do that" or "you will never be good enough". The resulting shift of thinking now sends a message that you can and you will; an internal dialogue now filled with life-giving words. This prison break now allows the overcomer to become a new creation (2 Corinthians 5:17) complete with a renewed mind (Romans 12:2).

Chains have been broken, the cell door has been unlocked and flung wide open; you are free! Nothing can hold you back now!

Chapter 11

Everything Can't Be
For Someday

Now that you've been set free, what's next? You've been imprisoned for so long that you've put the majority of your life on hold for a faraway *someday*. How often have you told yourself that your dream could come to pass *someday*? That you would start looking for a better job *someday?* That you would seek a relationship *someday*? How often do we make these promises to ourselves only to never follow up on them? Everything can't be for someday; there has to be some things for today as well.

I began to feel as if I was living each day just waiting for a someday. Someday when things were better. Someday when everything in my life was perfectly aligned. Someday my prayers would be answered. I was allowing too much of my life to be for someday and I was forgetting about *today*. I was just wasting my life as I waited; I needed to learn to live in the moment. Yes, I needed to think of what was coming, but I also needed to live right where I was, even if it wasn't where I wanted to be.

One of the greatest struggles for an overcomer is learning to be content even when things are not as you would like them to be. The discovery of how to get from here to there is vitally important for the overcomer because, without this knowledge, it is too easy to become discouraged as you live for one day in the far off future of *someday*. Let me remind you: it isn't about the destination, it's about the journey and all the wonderful things that you learn along it.

Often we know where we would like to be but don't always know how to get from here to there. There is often a gap between who we are right now and who we would like to be. On your voyage to overcoming, you will recognize that the journey of life is a process; there will never be a time when life is perfectly aligned. Life is messy and always will be. There will always be future goals towards which we are working but how do we learn to live while we are waiting? How do you live today as you work towards getting from here (where you are) to there (where you want to be)?

I cannot stress the importance of celebrating any and all victories regardless of size or importance as an overcomer, particularly when you are not where you want to be in life. Each victory builds upon the next as hope is stirred up by what God is doing in your life today. Overcomers learn to celebrate the here and now as they learn to live in the fire. Just because trials have forced you into the flames doesn't mean you have to stop living. Even though you find yourself in the valley, you cannot refuse to keep living as you wait for the promises. And while you're waiting, why not worship Him? Because, as an overcomer, you know that there are blessings in the dark places. In fact, there can be great blessings in the fire, you just might need to work a little harder to find them.

I can remember sitting in church services, listening to individuals who had already come out of the fire. There is little I like more than testimony time, except perhaps baptisms! But, as I sat and listened, I kept thinking how I longed to hear someone's testimony from the middle of the trial, while the fire was still burning hotly. I wanted—no, I needed—to know how they got from the pit to the mountaintop. No one ever shared a testimony like that, so here is mine.

Stop living for someday. Each day choose happiness, choose joy, choose whom you will serve. Don't waste the gift of today; find the good in every day. Be present today. Be in the moment. Enjoy the people you are with. Overcomers work towards their future *somedays* but don't dismiss the present days. Press in as you experience all He has for you, both the good and the bad. I know I've said this before, but I encourage you to enjoy the journey. Enjoy the process, not just the end result; enjoy who you are becoming. I had to remind myself of that while writing this chapter because I have a habit of plowing through everything; both degrees, the purchase of my home, graduations—you name it. I even felt as if I should plow through this book as I push ever forward. But then I was reminded by the Lord to enjoy the process of writing. I was reminded to relax, take a breath, and enjoy the lessons He was continuing to teach me as He molded me into His image.

I then felt an urge to take the time to examine who I was becoming in this process of writing and overcoming. I took a moment to examine how I was changing as I was becoming the version of me I was always meant to be. For an overcomer experiencing this, it's a pretty wild ride, filled with amazing new things each day as you learn to live for today rather than someday. Along the way, you also learn to count your blessings daily, reminding yourself that there is always something to rejoice in today. As an overcomer, I have learned that, even when it is difficult to be thankful, my default answer can always be "Thank you, Lord, that when you called, I answered". Honestly, and I'm sure you've heard this before, I may not be where I want to be but thank you, Lord, that I am not where I was!

Trials do not mean that life is over. You can still live while you are in the fire. Overcomers may have to remind themselves of these truths on occasion. I imagine that as you read those words, your budding overcomer's brain was shouting at me, "How?" I know I certainly asked that question on far more occasions than I would care to admit.

It may take some effort, but find and do what makes you happy. Do what gives you joy. Prepare for your next assignment. Rediscover yourself. Enjoy the people you are with in this season. Try new things; learn, grow, discover. Do something every day that you love to do. My advice to you: use the good china, buy the dress, or wear the shoes because this day was a someday at one point too. Engage in life and with people. A few simple things I do that bring great return on investment are fresh flowers on my kitchen windowsill. Yet another activity is what I call the trifecta of simple pleasures. I am obsessed with 3x5 notecards and washi tape—please don't ask me why—I cannot explain this—both are fortunately inexpensive. I purchase washi tape in my favorite colors, decorate the notecards, and use them to write down my memory verses. Adding simple joy in my day-to-day life! Find what works for you.

In the midst of life, you may still catch yourself waiting for your someday; that's fine. Dreams and hopes for a future are what excite us; they get us out of bed in the morning to greet the day with anticipation. Our best days are yet to be, but today can be pretty spectacular as well!

As you wait in your season of someday, remember there is still joy to be found. Remind yourself of this as often as necessary—this season will not last forever, there will be an end to it. Each day, purposefully increase the hope within you as you find the joy, learning to be content in your circumstances. Like Paul, find the joy in the trial and sing praises while imprisoned as you bring to mind the promises of your Heavenly Father. Stand firm in them. Just because it *hasn't* changed, doesn't mean it *won't*. Believe. Have faith.

This truly is the day that the Lord has made. I urge you to find a way in which to rejoice, because, overcomer, your someday is today!

Chapter 12

Being the Answer to Our Own Prayers

You've prayed, you've prepared, and now it's time to position yourself to receive those answered prayers. Often, our automatic thought is that the "amen" at the end our prayers is just that, the end. But what if it is only the beginning? There comes a time when you need to take your faith out and give it some exercise in preparation for taking a leap of faith.

One of my first leaps of faith involved what I thought to be an impossible dream: to own a home again. The apartment in which we were living no longer fit our needs, nor was there room in the budget for a mortgage, much less a down payment. So I prayed, and prayed. I asked friends and family to pray. To be completely open with you, this dream seemed impossible, but the longing within my heart would not let this dream go. I was a woman on a mission, determined that a house for my children and myself was going to become a reality.

I believe we can't keep waiting until everything in life is perfect; we all know that is never going to happen. We have to send our prayers heavenward, trusting that the Lord will hear and answer, and then...we jump! In the fall of 2013, I began saving every box I could get my hands on at work, bringing them home to stack them neatly at the entrance of my apartment. Every time I walked in or out of that door, I saw those boxes and reminded myself to believe that I was going to own a house one day. I kept praying and kept believing for that house as I continued to save those boxes. One day, I decided to take my prophetic act one step further: I was going to begin packing those boxes. So, in December of that same year, I began packing up my knick-knacks in the hope of moving. I kept looking at that stack of boxes, kept praying, and kept believing for my future house.

The next step toward this house was the actual search. I began my house search without actually believing it would result in anything. Even though I thought I was being so brave by engaging in these acts, I was still not fully committed to believing that my prayers would be answered in the affirmative, so I waited to call a realtor. In fact, I waited until March of 2014 to pick up the phone and make that call. One particular house caught my eye; I loved it and visualized my family living in it. Imagine my disappointment when the house was listed as under contract; it almost made me want to stop looking—but I did not. Within days, this very same house was back on the market; I thought for sure this was the house for me, only for it to go under contract with a different buyer.

Even though that was disheartening, I continued to look and pray, and then look some more. I would love to be able to tell you that I remained firm in my beliefs for this house, but I wavered, and while I was wavering I was worrying, too. For months, I worried about how I was ever going to be able to afford a house; wondered how I would handle any repairs; worried and wondered, and then worried some more. Then, one day, the Lord sent me a reminder—I imagine He had been sending me reminders for quite some time and I had just failed to hear His still, small voice. He reminded me that the funds were available and sitting in my bank account in the form of a larger-than-expected tax refund.

I believe that when you see the right house while house searching, you can call it home immediately. There was one house that I kept coming back to; I could imagine my family living there—I even imagined where my furniture would fit. I watched that house for weeks but never put in an offer because it was over my budget. Each time I searched for houses, I was drawn to this one. As I watched and waited, the price of this house dropped not just once, but twice! Needless to say, I picked up the phone and finally called my realtor.

There may be many times in your life when you need to put some action behind your prayers. By believing in the God of the impossible, you can take a supernatural step in the direction of your prayers even while it looks impossible in the natural. This doesn't only apply to a house, either; it could be prayers for anything. Ask yourself, *what can I do—here and now—to bring me one step closer to the request I have made of the Lord?* Then get ready to take that leap of faith!

Overcomers, we need to pray, prepare, and then position ourselves. Through our prayers we make our requests known. When waiting for answered prayers, we prepare to receive that answer by following His lead, and then position ourselves to receive that answer. You needn't see a logical explanation as to how these prayers will come about, you just need to pray confidently as only a child of the most High King can. Remember: "And all things, whatsoever ye shall ask in prayer, believing, ye shall receive" (Mathew 21:22, KJV).

As you pray, believing your prayers will be answered, your faith is being activated as you send Him the message that, even while you cannot see the answers in front of you, you are trusting Him to provide. Adding action—that leap of faith—to our prayers also sends God the message of just how serious we are about our requests. We do what we can through our own power and then rest in Him, waiting on His perfect timing.

I remember a very long, arduous season in which nothing I tried to do resulted in success. It was here that I learned to find rest in the waiting. I did what I could, then left the rest up to Him. Being the answer to your own prayer requires discernment as there is a fine line of knowing when to stop and when to go. You need to allow the still small voice of the Holy Spirit to prompt you. I like to say that you need to walk like an Egyptian—or, rather, like a Hebrew in Egypt during the Exodus—as you follow the leading of the Lord. Move only when He says move, and stop when He says stop. The Lord will reveal the next step at the exact moment that you need to take it.

While we're at it, keep in mind that your prayers may require some work on your part. This book wasn't going to write itself; I needed to sit down, plan it out, pray over it and then put some action behind all my prayers. I wrote, prayed, rewrote, prayed some more, and then rewrote yet again as I sought His direction. It didn't just happen because I wanted it to; I also had to be willing to put in the work to back up my prayers, reinforcing my belief that my prayers would be answered with some action on my part.

When we choose to live by what God says in His word—not seeing the expected results immediately—we stretch our faith muscles. As we hold tightly to the belief that our prayers will be answered, we can reinforce it by acting or speaking out in faith about what we believe will happen, much like saving boxes for a someday house. When we engage in such behavior, we begin to cultivate a spirit of expectation and hope. Saving boxes caused my expectations for a house to increase until they became a reality. I've applied this same concept to other prayers, as well. When I started a new job, I purchased a briefcase. At another time, I hung keys where I could see them, representing open doorways for opportunities that I was praying for.

This is goal setting 101: determine your goal, then do a reality check as you list all the steps that you need to take in order to achieve that goal. In a way, you are pre-writing history; writing it down before it happens, then working towards it. Some people post pictures of what they want, a process called treasure mapping or vision boarding. Our minds are very visual, so it actually helps our minds to see this "reality" before it is even created. We see those pictures and believe in our dreams a little more. Writing down and posting your goals is a good one too. When we break the job down into smaller parts, it no longer seems so overwhelming. Do something every day that gets you closer to a goal, even if you do it badly. Visualize yourself performing your dream, living in it, experiencing it. Every time you engage in this type of activity, it creates a snowball effect for both your future and your prayers. For the overcomer, building upon past victories increases your belief in future victories as you realize your track record with the Lord is pretty good. Keep a journal of your answered prayers as a reminder of how faithful He has been to you.

"Go to the ant, thou sluggard; consider her ways, and be wise" (Proverbs 6:6, KJV).

Now, let's get to work!

Chapter 13

Waiting in the Wilderness

"O God of my life, I'm lovesick for you in this weary wilderness" (Psalm 63:1, TPT).

By now, as an overcomer, you've found what you need in Jesus; you're most likely working on your trust and acceptance of love and to release yourself from your mental prisons, and you have begun your search for the beauty to be birthed from the ashes of your life. Yet you still find yourself waiting and waiting, and then, quite possibly, waiting some more. You've done all you can; now you must wait for things that have changed in the supernatural to catch up to the natural.

With the fire beginning to die down, you may find yourself chomping at the bit as you wait for permission from the Lord to move forward into your destiny. You know something amazing is coming, and you can't wait for it to get here. This anticipation, this eagerness for your destiny, becomes all you think about most days. Yet, still, you wait.

Throughout this time, you need to take care to keep your eyes focused on the Lord, as well as to live in the moment and not focus only on what's coming in the future. For an overcomer, this is the perfect time to make those final preparations for what the Lord has been teaching you. As you rest and wait in Him, use this time to be sure everything is ready for what's coming, especially you.

In my season of waiting, I also learned that I didn't need to act out of desperation. For me, this season was one of unemployment, and I was becoming quite concerned over finances (okay, frantic might be a more accurate description). Logic told me I should be more concerned over my situation than I was as it pushed me towards applying for any positions I was even remotely qualified for. But, somewhere deep within me, I was relaxed. I wasn't all that worried. Sure, I had moments here and there where the fears were manifested, but they were only moments because, by now, I had learned how to do battle against such thoughts and would quickly turn them into praise about how much I loved and trusted my Heavenly Father to know best. It didn't take long for those thoughts to disappear with that approach. Short prayers of "Okay, what's the next step?" or "What do I need to do about this?" were also helpful.

The natural told me I should be filled with fear, but the spiritual told me I could rest in His promises as I waited for the end of this wilderness season and the beginning of the next. The dilemma was often where to find this rest when one is weary and worn; where can this life-giving water be found? In this time, relax, breathe, and trust. Engage in some heartfelt praise and worship as you draw closer to God. This is your time to learn to wait, to develop your patience as you trust His perfect timing. You learn to lean into the waiting and relax.

As I continued in the holding pattern I was in, I was learning patience and perseverance as the Lord taught me where to find the life-giving water I so desperately needed for survival—in Him. Here I learned to seek Him when He seemed most distant, as He was just waiting for me to take my turn at searching Him out. At this time, I learned that He is always with me, and will never leave me. Here, I learned to seek Him until I found Him, and, when I found Him, determined to never let Him go again. Throughout this season, I also learned to trust His perfect timing, reminding myself that God was in the waiting with me. Here I also discovered that God was providing manna each day for my needs. This manna may not have looked as I expected, or may not have even been what I wanted, but it was always exactly what I needed. Here, I learned to wait "...patiently for the Lord; and he inclined unto me, and heard my cry" (Psalm 40:1, KJV).

As we remember that He will hear our cry, we can also remember that each season is just that—a season—and, as such, it will have a beginning and an end. As part of my cry, I needed to ask for faith to see me through the dry wilderness-season of waiting. When you reach this point, overcomer, you will need to decide to trust as you rest in His promises because there is no need for striving in this season. Here, you can choose to experience the peace of the Lord that passes all understanding as He provides for your every need. We may only see wasteland before us, but all God sees is potential for an oasis; a truth that holds true for many situations in our life.

As you await His promises to come, retreat to be with Him; get away from the world and take your focus off of your problems. You may only see the impossibility of the desert in front of you, but hope and faith can still be found. It is when you come to the end of yourself that you will find Him. There are times when God calls us to this place of seclusion in order that we might learn to be alone with Him—that we might learn to see and hear Him clearly. It is during the waiting in the wilderness that you learn to sing a new song, a song that will now harmonize perfectly with His. Sometimes God has to take away the noise of life just so you can hear Him.

This season in the wilderness may leave us feeling alone as we silently wait, but it is within this waiting that we build our confidence that He will come back. Throughout this time in the desert, we eagerly learn to expect His return, longing for His presence, learning to stop and go at His command, trusting His direction at every turn. In this wilderness, our heart becomes so entwined with His that we voluntarily submit our will to His. In the desert, we stop striving to do things in our own power and patiently wait in His presence.

Throughout this waiting, take a moment to examine to what you are clinging. What is it that you continually refuse to release that He has asked you to? On my journey towards overcoming, I seemed to spend a rather long time in this season as a nomad with no place to call home; I had to wonder if some of this was of my own doing. Was I doing something—or not doing something—that was prolonging my time in the wilderness?

There is no doubt that the dry, dusty season in the wilderness is a challenge as you long for His refreshing presence. You learn to hear God's voice the clearest because all else is removed and it's only you and the Lord. You learn what you don't need and how to let go of the unnecessary. In this season, you grow closer to Him as you seek Him more; learning to rely on Him; to depend, rest, and trust in Him.

It is this rest in which the overcomer can take a few relaxing breaths as they place all of their concerns in His more than capable hands. What they see before them makes no sense in the natural, logical world, but God isn't based on logic. It is human nature to resist the new; time spent in this season teaches the overcomer to stop the struggling and welcome what the Lord is doing as a harvest of great spiritual growth begins.

Alone in the wilderness, you may begin to question your mind, your sanity, even your reality as, at times, what God is asking of you makes no sense. You may question if it was truly God you heard, or if you can trust Him in all of this; wondering how your life will work out along the way to your final destination. Then, like in Exodus, He will provide the direction during both night and day.

This season brings about a greater intimacy with the Lord, which, eventually, will help you guide others through their personal wilderness journeys. Your trials increase your compassion for others as a result of this season—a compassion you will one day use to minister to them. In this season, in spite of all you might lack, an attitude of gratitude develops as you see Him more clearly in more and more areas of life. The wilderness season also teaches you to have less fear towards the unknown and as a result, greatly reduces any hold fear may have over you. As you move on after each battle, you are well on your way to becoming a seasoned warrior because you have learned, "He that dwelleth in the secret place of the most High shall abide under the shadow of the Almighty" (Psalm 91:1, KJV). You are safe, secure, and always on the lookout for what God might be trying to teach you.

Even in the uncertainty of the wilderness, the overcomer can live confidently as she fully believes that God will follow through on His promises. Slowly, she learns that even when she is struck down by trials in life, she will not be destroyed; she is becoming more than a conqueror. In this season of dryness, beautiful overcomers learn to do more than survive—do more than just get by— and they learn to thrive in spite of the lack. Here in the wilderness, the overcomer learns to stand firm on Scriptures, promises, and prophecies. Here she learns her trials are not just for her edification, but also for the edification of others in their own wilderness seasons.

If we take the time to look around the wilderness, we notice the many bones lying about. It is here that many lose their focus as they take their eyes off of Jesus. The loneliness becomes too much, or perhaps it is the sacrifices required by the waiting that cause people to quit. The season seems unending, and the overcomer questions if her prayers truly have been heard. Have her tears been shed in vain? Surely this dryness will never end.

She cries out to God, wondering where He is and why He has yet to answer her prayers.

This wilderness may feel like the darkest of nights to the wandering soul, but, as an overcomer, you have a choice: you can turn to God or you can turn from Him. If you hold on, there will come a brokenness that leads to complete surrender. This may sound terrifying initially, but give it time. God has promised that He will breathe into your dry bones; trust that when He does so, "…ye shall live; and ye shall know that I *am* the Lord" (Ezekiel 37:6, KJV). Keep in mind, God is using this time to teach you and while you may feel alone or as if death is preferable, He is actually sheltering and protecting you as He prepares you for the next season.

Take heart; there is still growth in the wilderness. Trust in the faithfulness of His promises while you wait for this season to end. In Ecclesiastes 3:1 we read, "To every thing there is a season, and a time to every purpose under the heaven" (KJV). Trust that, even though your life is not in perfect alignment, it is safe to trust, obey, and wait patiently for the Lord to move, because He will, without a doubt!

Rest in knowing that the Father has all things under control and is working them out for your good. Press in. Learn to be still in His presence. Let Him be Lord. We are reminded in Scriptures, "But they that wait upon the LORD shall renew their strength; they shall mount up with wings as eagles; they shall run, and not be weary; and they shall walk, and not faint" (Isaiah 40:31, KJV). Dig a little deeper, find the strength to persevere. Learn to rest in the waiting, He will reward your diligence.

SHERRY LYNN

Chapter 14

Spiritual Warriors Stand Firm in Storms

Picture this: a lone individual is standing on a cliff by a stormy sea. Flashes of lightning illuminate the dark sky as the waves crash over the rocks below; causing the cold sea spray to drench her. The torrential downpour renders her dark blue rain coat ineffective, and, as a result of the storm, she is unable to stand upright. But, rather than scurrying for shelter, she leans into the wind. She presses forward as she rests securely in the knowledge of who has her back.

We are often distracted by the turmoil surrounding us, causing us to take our eyes off of Jesus as we focus on the storm, much like Peter in the book of Matthew. And, much like Peter, the moment I took my eye from Jesus, I began to sink. Just like Peter, I cried out to the Lord to save me, "And immediately Jesus stretched forth his hand, and caught him, and said unto him, O thou of little faith, wherefore didst thou doubt?" (Matthew 14:31, KJV). Why do we let the wind and the waves distract us?

Overcomer, the storms are going to come and in order to survive them, you will need to stand firm as you learn to approach the tempest like a warrior training for battle. With each storm comes fresh strategies for battle, allowing you, as the overcoming warrior, to exercise newly acquired skills and weapons. With each storm, as well as each subsequent victory, you develop greater strength and confidence in your fighting skills as well. These storms might knock you off course but trust that God will bring you to an even greater destination.

Thunder may startle us with all its noise, but by itself it is quite harmless. I think of it much like a distraction tactic of the enemy as he makes yet another feeble attempt to get our eyes off of Jesus. By learning to rest in the storm, to lean into it, trusting that the Lord has our back, we can wear out the enemy. If we remain focused on Jesus, there is no way—even with all the noise around us—that we can be defeated. If we ignore the threats of being pulled under by the storm, we can find rest and peace in our guarantee of a victorious outcome as we fight, not worrying whether or not we will win, because we know that we cannot lose.

When you are barely holding on as the storm rages all about you, how do you dig a little deeper? What do you do in those moments when your faith has been stretched to the breaking point and there is barely any strength left to fight the latest attack? How do you pray one more prayer when you haven't seen any answers in ages? Where do you get that much-needed faith in those moments?

Within the storm we can find the still, small voice capable of calming the waves. By focusing on Jesus in spite of the storm raging around us, we can be strengthened by God's faithfulness, as we remain steadfast until victorious. Remember, "For the Lord your God is he that goeth with you, to fight for you against your enemies, to save you" (Deuteronomy 20:4, KJV). As I learn that the battle has already been won and that I'm on the winning side, I can withstand any storm.

Often, battles call for a strategy that requires the warrior to keep her head down, moving ever-forward in the face of adversity and uncertainty. The majority of the trials and tests sent our way require that we stand firm, not quitting as the enemy makes yet another feeble attempt to keep us from pursuing our purpose. During this violent battle weather, you may feel as if your faith is breaking rather than stretching. I believe that the closer you are to the mark, the more opposition will come your way. We must be doing something right if the attacks of the enemy are increasing! Rather than hide for safety when the storms increase, we need to press in and stand firm.

How we approach these storms plays a role in how they impact us as it is our attitude that can make them destructive or beneficial. As we stand firm, preparing for the next level, we approach the battle from a place of victory, firmly believing that the Lord will protect and shelter us. The battle may rage so fiercely that all your strength is required to simply hold your ground. You may not advance much, but it still counts as a victory. With your focus firmly on Christ, you will not be tossed about by the waves of your circumstances. Scriptures remind us:

"Have not I commanded thee? Be strong and of good courage; be not afraid, neither be thou dismayed; for the Lord thy God is with thee whithersoever thou goest" (Joshua 1:9, KJV).

As warriors remember past battles, they build on those victories, keeping in mind that, "I can do all things through Christ which strengtheneth me" (Philippians 4:13, KJV). Warriors also remember that when they are faced with fear, their trust can be put in the Lord (Psalm 56:3). Previous wins have prepared the spiritual warrior to go before the soldiers, holding the front lines until reinforcements can arrive. As these warriors, we forge new territory, taking back land that the enemy had previously stolen from us.

There will be times when reinforcements are necessary in order to win the battle. These may take the form of a secret weapon, something I call *spiritual superpowers.* Throughout my countless battles I have come to realize my superpower comes in the form of my words; it's how I beat back the enemy. There have been battles when I've repeatedly fought back by saying the same phrase each time the enemy tried an attack, and there have been other battles that I've won by posting my encouraging words on social media as I use its powers for good, encouraging brothers and sisters in the Lord fighting similar battles. Regardless of what your spiritual superpower is—once you discover it—you will be unbeatable!

Another valuable strategy has been the confidence gained by my knowledge that neither God nor I am going anywhere; we are both in the battle to the end. When the battles of life look impossible, I remind myself that I've already won. Because of this knowledge, I can then encourage others in their faith as they face their own battles. Due to my security in Christ I know— that no matter how dangerous my stormy circumstances may be—I can experience assurance knowing His help is on the way.

There will be days when there is a break in the battle, allowing you to catch your breath as you prepare for the next fight. On these days you can take a moment and look back over your past victories. As you do, you will realize how strong you have become and stand a little taller. Take a deep breath, square your shoulders, and get ready for the next onslaught, only this time you have a secret weapon—trustworthiness. You know that God has fought your battles with you in the past and He will continue to do so in the future.

As an overcomer, you have learned to celebrate the small victories. You no longer worry about how quickly you are progressing; instead your focus has become on who you are becoming. On those particularly difficult days, you count getting up in the morning as a victory; standing firm counts as a victory. You've looked back, realized all you've walked through to get to this point, and taken a breath. Wow, you really have come a long way!

There were many mornings when I woke up feeling as if the battle had already begun and I needed to put on my armor in order to perform the simplest of tasks. Wielding our sword and carrying a shield should come as no surprise as Scriptures warn us: "For we wrestle not against flesh and blood, but against principalities, against powers, against the rulers of the darkness of this world, against spiritual wickedness in high places" (Ephesians 6:12, KJV).

Often, untried warriors experience a panic which threatens to overwhelm them; this is another well-used tactic of the enemy. When this happens, remind him—and yourself—that you possess the power to still the storm and as such cannot be overwhelmed because of who your God is! Because you belong to the King, the very Creator of the universe, the same resurrection power that raised Jesus from the grave also resides within you. When you whisper *"peace, be still"* to the storm (Mark 4:39, KJV), it must obey due to the power and authority behind your words. In fact, one of the greatest arsenals we possess is Scripture; praying these words in the face of adversity wields great power.

The warrior may find that each storm attempts to outdo the last one as the enemy becomes more and more fearful of your ever increasing strength in battle. Because of this, he may begin to send more and more attacks in your direction. I like to say, that when we experience attacks like this, we have the enemy running scared and must be doing something right! This onslaught of storms feels as if destruction is imminent, but it really isn't. God is actually using each of these storms to impart valuable battle strategies to you. The enemy sends storms to distract you, but, by keeping our eyes on Jesus, they have minimal effect. The harder the enemy attacks, the more we can rest safely under His wings. We are reminded, "He that dwelleth in the secret place of the most High shall abide under the shadow of the Almighty" (Psalm 91:1, KJV).

Another thing to remember about these storms is that they only last for a season and will eventually come to an end. Much like the individual standing on the rocks in my dream, we can learn to lean into the storm, basing our security on the relationship we have previously built with Jesus. We know that we are not alone in the storm and that due to His presence, we can find peace while the stormy battles rage all around us. Hunker down, and stand firm!

We are reminded to "Be strong and of a good courage, fear not, nor be afraid of them: for the LORD thy God, he it is that doth go with thee; he will not fail thee, nor forsake thee" (Deuteronomy 31:6, KJV). Maintaining this courage as a warrior will allow you to thrive in the face of the hardships of battle. Overcomers, don't discount yourself in the storms, you can still do great things while in the fiery trials of life.

In every overcomer's journey there comes a time when these battles must be taken seriously as the enemy seeks to destroy you as a believer in Christ. Scriptures warn us of our enemy: "Be sober, be vigilant; because your adversary the devil, as a roaring lion, walketh about, seeking whom he may devour" (1 Peter 5:8, KJV). These battles may occur daily—even without our realization—but realize that they are happening! As an overcomer, you need to prepare for war! Fight for blessing and breakthrough; fight knowing that you are not alone.

All overcomers, just like all warriors, must engage in training in preparation for battle. Your greatest weapons may come in the most surprising forms. One is rest, which we've already talked about. A second is learning to wield the sacrifice of praise. Praise carries a lot of power and can be used to defeat the enemy as well as bolstering the warrior's heart. Scriptures state, "By him therefore let us offer the sacrifice of praise to God continually, that is, the fruit of our lips giving thanks to his name" (Hebrews 13:15, KJV). Yet another weapon is wielded through our prayers; when our prayers are combined with persistence, they can defeat even the strongest enemy.

The use of Scriptures as a weapon in conjunction with words is amazingly effective. First, the spoken word carries with it the power to bring life or death. This is paramount in fighting these battles. But, more importantly, when God's word is spoken over our battles, overcomers give Him the ability to bring life into that situation. When combined, prayer, Scripture, and persistence make the warrior unbeatable in any battle.

Warrior-overcomers are to enforce the victory already won on the cross by confidently meeting the powers of darkness. Because of the power of Christ within us, we have the power to overcome the darkness and are qualified to represent Jesus in this battle. We read in Scriptures, "But if the Spirit of him that raised up Jesus from the dead dwell in you, he that raised up Christ from the dead shall also quicken your mortal bodies by his Spirit that dwelleth in you" (Romans 8:11, KJV). As we enforce what Christ has done on the cross, we also enforce His victory, gaining valuable experience that will, in turn, come to the aid of newly enlisted warrior-overcomers.

Beware, warriors; the enemy may engage in covert attacks as he uses his weapon of distraction, slowly creeping into our minds while we remain oblivious. How many times have you experienced one of those days in which you wander about aimlessly, unable to concentrate or put your finger on what is unsettling you? This is just one example of distraction as the enemy attempts to pull you in any direction except the one on which you need to focus.

Double agents may arrive in the form of lies. We may think we are being defeated and crushed by the enemy as he brings discouragement into our battle field. Losing hope or taking our eyes off Jesus causes us to quickly become disheartened as fear of failure creeps in. Stay steadfast! Look for encouragement in little love notes from the Lord that take the form of messages from home to a battle weary soldier; such as the perfect song or verse or word that is spoken just when you need to hear it most.

Discouragement was one of my greatest battles. When I lost hope or took my eyes off of Jesus, I would (and continue to) quickly become disheartened as fear filled my thoughts, but then something would come into my life to encourage me; one of those sweet love notes from my Heavenly Father that bolster my faith. With the Lord by your side, you are already a victor! No matter what battles you may face, continue on, overcomer; you are on the winning side.

All is not lost, warrior; as you increase your warfare tactics, you will learn of the serious nature of these battles, and, in the process, learn to take yourself and your abilities more seriously. The battle we find ourselves fighting in is real. You cannot back down and must fight with persistence as you hold the frontlines until reinforcements arrive.

We are in a battle with the greatest enemy we will ever face: an opponent who is highly skilled in the most effective techniques known to man (techniques he's perfected through use over hundreds of years). But you are fighting a battle that you cannot lose because it has already been fought and won on the cross by Jesus. Remember, you have fought the good fight, you have finished the course, and you have kept the faith (2 Timothy 4:7, KJV). There is no reason to quit; you are already an overcomer based on Jesus, plain and simple. Because of Jesus you are victorious; because of Jesus you will overcome.

Chapter 15

Forgiveness

I'm going to call this a KISS chapter because we're going to *keep it simple, sweetie.*

Forgiveness—let's be honest, we all want it, but are we willing to give it? In Scriptures we are told that if we confess our sins, we will be forgiven and cleansed (1 John 1:9). We are also told to forgive others because of that very same forgiveness we have received (Matthew 6:14-15). We are then reminded in Matthew 18:22 that we are to forgive our brother not just once, but multiple times; seventy times seven to be exact. Within the Christian community, the topic of forgiveness is often forced on believers, and they may find themselves coerced into offering forgiveness prematurely or have an unclear understanding of what it is that forgiveness entails.

Forgiveness isn't always easy. There may be times when an offender demands your forgiveness without an apology or admission of guilt—what then? An offender may not deserve your forgiveness—what do you do in circumstances like these?

What about an offender who has never even asked for forgiveness—how is a believer to handle these situations? We are to forgive others as we have been forgiven. There is no question of that, but what is often overlooked when forgiving another is that forgiveness is not equal to forgetting, nor does it automatically mean reconciliation, as there may be occasions when continuing the relationship will put the individual in harm's way.

Forgiveness is also a process complete with multiple layers; on your way to overcoming, I suggest forgiving as much as you are able to in that moment. Because when you forgive, you aren't just forgiving the offender; you also forgive for your benefit. In the act of forgiving, you will be set free and allowed to move on from the offence. Overcomers know that forgiveness equals freedom; by extending grace and forgiveness—even if their offender is undeserving—they are released from the shackles of unforgiveness.

Here's the interesting thing about forgiveness: as mentioned above, it is a process and may take more than one act of forgiving. In many instances, I have found that greater levels of forgiveness will develop over time. You forgive as much as you can now, trusting that more—and eventually complete—forgiveness will come later. When you have grown as an overcomer and are more able to forgive, you can and will forgive to the next level. The freeing that occurs when we forgive removes a barrier between you and the Lord, allowing for a deeper relationship with the Father as He reveals more of His heart towards you. Grace and mercy come into play, breaking down those barriers that keep you from loving relationships between yourself and your peers, as well as between you and the Lord. Overcomers follow the promptings of the Holy Spirit, surprising themselves with words of forgiveness that they never thought to utter.

Here is one woman's short story of how forgiveness freed her:

> Freedom is found in forgiveness as you look in the teary eyes of your former abuser while his father lies dying on a hospital bed. Your only thought is to minister to him because the love of the Father overpowers every other emotion. The words that come from your lips are Spirit-spoken as freedom is found.

Through this experience, the woman in the story gained a greater understanding of the depth to which her Heaven Father had forgiven her. As she underwent this act of forgiving her offender, she, as an overcomer, learned firsthand how to forgive as she had been forgiven. Through this amazing story, she forgave at a previously unimaginable level. Extending this forgiveness to her undeserving abuser broke the ties that were holding her back. Any power or control her abuser may have held over her was removed as a result of this simple act; an act which freed her to experience even greater forgiveness from her Heavenly Father. No longer could unforgiveness hold her back, just like it will no longer hold you back once you forgive.

Let's also remember that we need to forgive ourselves as well. I've spoken with numerous individuals who just cannot receive release from the guilt and unforgiveness towards themselves that they continuously carry around with them. The grace we extend to others is also available to us; be as kind to yourself as you would be towards a friend. No one is ever so far gone from God or so immersed in their sin that forgiveness is not available. You can come before His throne just as you are and He will greet you with open arms. When God looks at you, He doesn't see all of your sins; if you've accepted Christ as your Savior, all He sees is that you have been washed clean by the blood of Jesus.

The lifestyle choice of forgiveness will be liberating for you as an overcomer; many unexpected doors will open as a result of this choice. Overcomers who obediently follow the commandment to forgive will be unshackled; this unshackling frees them to enter into the next level of their Jesus-walk. Even after years of being a Jesus-follower, new levels of forgiveness may be achieved as you experience this newfound freedom in forgiveness.

I encourage you to forgive as you have been forgiven.

Chapter 16

Fear is a Lie

I'm going to take a moment here to be completely vulnerable. There are mornings when my first waking thoughts are not filled with "thank you, Jesus, for today", but are rather filled with fear: fear of the unknown, fear of finances, fear of the future, even fear of success! My heart pounds, my stomach churns, my blood pressure rises, and it isn't even 8:00 AM! I know, crazy, right?

Wait, I'm not alone? You're right there with me on this one?

But why? Why do we continue to be afraid when God has proven His faithfulness to us over and over? Why do we allow fear to control us when we know that it just holds us back? Because, if we're really honest with ourselves, those fears we allow to rob us of so much joy never seem to amount to much of anything, do they?

Fear truly has no place in the life of an overcomer. Join me for a moment; let's examine this a little more. When we finally gather the courage to face our fears and allow the door of change to be opened, we realize how very small those fears have been all along. As we realize the majority of our fears are not based on truth but rather on lies of the enemy, intended to hold us back, it changes everything.

For too long we've been slaves to our fears and have allowed them to restrain and chain us. So very much of what we are afraid of is our own making; the majority of our fear is actually an issue of trust as we fail to believe in the Lord's capabilities. Fear is a tactic of the enemy, one which he is quite skilled at wielding. The same enemy will use fear as a smokescreen; sending you the message that what you are afraid of is bigger than God, much like an idol overshadowing His place and power in your life. Fear makes us question in whose image we are created.

Overcomers need to examine the reason behind their fears, as well as what is causing this fear to overshadow the glorious strength that is waiting to lift them up each day. We read in Scriptures: "There is no fear in love; but perfect love casteth out fear: because fear hath torment. He that feareth is not made perfect in love" (I John 4:18, KJV). Don't forget that we, as believers in Christ, are on the winning side.

What exactly is it that we are so afraid of? The simple fear of stepping out of our comfort zone goes a long way to hinder us from reaching our full potential and realizing our dreams. Sometimes success is scary. Sometimes it isn't fear of failure that hinders us, but fear of success because we have become so accustomed to being unsuccessful. Stepping into the unknown is another fear that many struggle with. After all, someone might see how flawed and human we are; what happens then?

Our forward motion may be hindered by fear as we remain imprisoned in cages of our own design. Fear lies as it exclaims "no, you can't!" to any new ideas we throw in its direction. The journey towards our hopes and dreams has been delayed as we give fear entirely too much power over our actions. Fear is propaganda placed strategically in our lives by the enemy, causing us to put our trust in anything *but* God. Why do we allow this lie to continue its negative influence over our lives? Why don't we put our foot down and say "no more"?

Every overcomer reaches the point in which they say *enough*; enough of fear's lies holding me back—enough! You decide that fear will no longer prevent your forward movement, or cause you to be ineffective; no longer will fear immobilize you! Referring back to that Joseph Campbell quote: "The cave you fear to enter holds the treasure you seek", but that which we are most afraid of is also what we most desire. There is nothing that dishonest, two-faced, lying enemy we battle would like more than to hold us back from our destiny.

There are two types of fear: healthy and unhealthy. In order to determine whether a specific fear is of the unhealthy sort, you must first examine it to determine if its origins are based in truth or lies. Some fears are very healthy and protect us from harm. For example, jumping off a cliff or facing a robber who broke into your home should make us tremble in fear. But other fears, particularly those of the unhealthy nature, are based on condemnation rather than conviction. These fears do not protect;

they only harm. These fears are the reminders of all your failures, telling you not to try that new thing. These fears need to be kicked to the curb!

Our minds have made that fear larger than it really is, given it too much power to control us, and made us forget that it can be overcome. Remember on whose side we are and to whom we belong. Once you face your fears, you realize they aren't so scary after all. Is it easy? Nope! But it is certainly doable. Overcomers have realized that fears can be faced; we can do things *and* be afraid. We can be afraid and still move forward; tasks can be accomplished even in the face of fear. Fear may always be there but it doesn't have to control us or stop us from succeeding.

I imagine that, by now, you are nodding your head in agreement, sitting on the edge of your seat and eagerly awaiting the magnificent revelation coming your way to dispel all of your fears. Well, here goes: **silence the lies of the enemy with truth as he stirs up your fear**. When the enemy stirs up your fears, press into a deeper relationship with the Lord as you seek new revelation concerning those fears; ask the Lord to illuminate the roots of those fears, including the lies upon which they are based; fight back with promises from Scripture as you allow God's perfect love to cast out all your fears.

As an overcomer rests in these truths, the fear-filled lies of the enemy will be exposed. Overcomers may find an infinitesimal portion of their fears to be based in truth. For example, fear of lack of finances kept me in an inadequate living arrangement for far too long and held my family back from moving forward in our new life. When my car broke down and needed to be replaced, fear of purchasing a car on my own, without a man to help me, held me back. I had no idea how to find a trustworthy garage or a car dealer, but the Lord guided me to everything I needed. I found the car, the car dealer, and the garage in a single stop. It was the same with buying a house; I never thought I could do that on my own. In fact, I complained quite often to the Lord about that as well, until He finally showed me that I was perfectly capable of making such a purchase. Was it scary? Was I afraid? It certainly was, but I managed to get through it, and I found that, the more I faced these fears and just plowed right through them, the less power they held over me.

Remember: nothing is impossible for our God. When a fear is conquered, we are taught a lesson in trusting God, allowing us to conquer even more fears as we eventually learn to live life unafraid. Living unafraid consists of discerning between healthy and unhealthy fears as well as confronting our fears as we move into the unknown, trusting the Lord with the outcome. Living unafraid aids us in stepping into our destiny, and it also helps in coming before the throne of God boldly. Fearless living entails a lack of fear over failing; as doors of opportunity are opened overcomers are not afraid to walk through them and into the unknown.

There are times, I believe, when the fear signifies that we are on the right track; we've got the enemy scared and he's throwing all he's got at us in order to hinder our progress. Again, simply wielding our greatest weapon—truth—will repel those lie-arrows directly back to the enemy. Also, remember that sense of fear is just a feeling, and, as such, is not always accurate. In these times, I pull up all those memory verses to remind both myself and the enemy just who my God really is. One of my tried and true verses when faced with this type of attack is "What time I am afraid, I will trust in thee" (Psalm 56:3, KJV). It was one of the many verses I taught my children when they were younger, and it has stayed with me ever since, being brought to mind by the Holy Spirit when I need to squash one of those nasty fears.

Here's another truth to throw at the enemy when he attacks you in this manner: fear has already been overcome by the greatest overcomer of all times—Jesus. Fear was defeated on the cross; we no longer need to be afraid. This is a truth that the enemy works diligently to keep hidden from us because he doesn't want us to realize that these fears are mere smokescreens and have no real effect on us.

Once you face one fear, putting the next one in its place is a little easier. Ask yourself the magic question; instead of *what if my fears are real*, ask *what if they aren't?* What happens not *if* I overcome them, but *when*? What does that mean for me? The more you expose these fears as lies, the easier your work becomes.

Here's another truth: you and I are His for all eternity, but we don't have to wait until eternity to experience His peace and love—we can have that here and now, even in the face of fear. Lay down your fear and pick up Jesus; refuse to allow fear to have the power to paralyze you. Move forward even when afraid. That's right, that one is worth repeating; *you can do it afraid!* As an overcomer, you have resurrection power within you that can crush your fears. You never need to fear because the Lord is with you and you never walk alone; "I sought the LORD, and he heard me, and delivered me from all my fears" (Psalm 34:4, KJV).

Chapter 17

Life is Messy, but I'm Fine

How are you doing today?

Did you just answer me with "I'm fine"? Are you truly fine today?

At any given moment in our lives, there is a multitude of crises occurring: bills, home or car repairs, health issues, a prodigal child— the list could go on. The point here is that nothing is neat and orderly about life; it doesn't fit into a box, nor does it come wrapped with a bow. I think we all know this, yet we continue to pretend otherwise and attempt to present a perfect life to the world. We expend so much energy working to make our lives appear flawless that we fail to recognize just how beautiful our messy lives can be.

Each time I was asked "How are you?" my answer was always "fine". Every struggle, every conversation, every hurt was quietly tucked away for no one to see as I continued to answer with the lie that I was fine even though I wasn't. This went on for so long that I trained myself to minimize everything about me; I imagine I'm not alone in that behavior. Perhaps we tell people we are fine because we are trying to convince ourselves that we are. Continuing to provide the answer of "I'm fine" allows us to remain invisible and in hiding; by doing so, we attempt to avoid dealing with what a truthful answer may bring as others see us for the flawed person we are. How do we live life openly in such a critical world? By tossing this need for perfection out with the garbage!

Oh, that's not the answer you were looking for?

If you are like me, your search for perfection has lasted most of your life. Now, there are times when perfection is quite useful, and there are times when it is not. Too often, perfection damages our ability to be real, in turn hindering true intimacy in our relationships, including the one with our Heavenly Father. Perfection causes us to miss out on much in life as we become obsessed with cleaning, exercising, advancing, or are off in search of yet another goal; forgetting about the people in our lives. For years, we have given perfection permission to hide our humanness, but now I wonder: how many genuine relationships do we miss out on because we are too focused on hiding the real us?

Why do we give this topic so much power over us? Doesn't the endless pursuit of perfection seem similar to a hamster running on its wheel? Yet we continue to pursue it.

As an overcomer, we need to let go of presenting the perfect plastic life, particularly in the Christian crowd. Come on, we all know that we do it. The Sundays when you enter the church building with a smile on your face when not five minutes ago you were arguing with your spouse or reprimanding a naughty child. Those times you answer with "I'm fine" when your life is crumbling around you. Be real. Be authentic. Be yourself.

I will be the first to admit: I like things neat and tidy. There's a little joke in our house that when one of my children asks me how I want them to do a certain chore, the answer will be *alphabetically by color,* because, honestly, that's how I like things to look. Perfect, just like a house from a magazine; as if no one really lives there. But, that's not real, is it? Trust me, I tried to achieve that. When my two children were young, I spent the majority of my day cleaning and picking up after them, working late into the night to organize the house or bake at the holidays, putting toys away the moment they were set aside as I tried to present my family as ideal. And that was only the part of my life you could see; what about all the other skeletons in the closet I also worked so diligently to keep hidden: the disobedient, defiant children, or the arguments with my then-husband? To this day, I still question our need to hide our humanness.

Stop wasting so much time and energy in an attempt to gain the unobtainable goal of perfection. After all, don't our standards of perfection just set us up for failure? Working towards a standard of excellence is healthier and can actually help us reach greater achievements, while perfection, due to its impossible requirements, sets us up for failure. Let's give ourselves permission to relax and just be perfectly imperfect as we share our flaws openly. Trust that Jesus will meet you right where you are, in the very middle of your less-than-perfect life.

When we are in Christ, we can let go of the need for perfection. We can let go of the constant drive to achieve an impossible standard and learn to just be. We are complete in Him, which is not the same as being perfect. In Him, we can make the mistakes because, in Him, grace covers us. Scriptures remind us, "... my grace is sufficient for thee: for my strength is made perfect in weakness. Most gladly therefore will I rather glory in my infirmities, that the power of Christ may rest upon me" (2 Corinthians 12:9, KJV). When we are less than perfect, we can turn to Him, ask forgiveness, and move on as we allow His grace to cover us.

Admit it: there are skeletons in everyone's closet but it is often shame that keeps them there unnecessarily. We attempt to hide our messy lives, thinking that the lives of others are perfect and that they have it all together, when in reality their lives are just as messy as ours. Because of this we allow the weight of shame to keep us from living life authentically while we keep others at arm's length. This, in turn, causes us to miss out on experiencing true relationship. Pretending that life isn't filled with messiness is just ignoring the elephant in the room: it does not cause it to disappear. Shame over the messiness of our lives is just another of those tools used by the enemy to keep us under control because it allows him to hold us back from becoming who we were created to be. When we are open about our mistakes and sin, guilt and shame have no place in our lives. Now, I'm not saying we should talk about every sin to every person we meet, that could just prove disastrous. Be selective in who meets those skeletons of shame hidden deeply within your closet, but do allow some to be introduced.

Here's a thought: maybe your imperfections will be used to reach others for Christ. What if those flaws we work so hard to hide actually end up being what brings a lost individual to Christ? Wow! Maybe an open, honest dialogue concerning our imperfections will bring a lost sheep into God's fold. Why not begin a conversation on one of those uncomfortable topics? It just might set someone free from their burden of shame. My opinion is that the church, as well as its members, are in need of conducting an honest conversation concerning their skeletons. We could begin with a few conversations on abuse, adultery, abortion, or addiction that just might set some people free of their guilt and shame—and that's only the first letter of the alphabet. Face it, we all mess up; we all sin. "For all have sinned, and come short of the glory of God" (Romans 3:23, KJV); it's how you deal with that sin that matters most. Ask for forgiveness and move on.

The funny thing about that guilt and shame is that we allow it to hold us back from so much. We allow these feelings to place chains upon our wrists and ankles. Then, we mistakenly think these chains are so strong that nothing can break them, letting them tie us down until our lives end. But didn't Jesus die on the cross to set us free from things like this? His redemptive work on the cross saved us from hell, but his death also freed us from those restraints as well.

The enemy wants you to remain chained to this misconception that life is too messy to be shared in hopes that you will remain firmly shackled to shame. He wants you to carry that shame and guilt over your humanness, he wants you to try to hide your very you-ness because he actually is quite afraid of what you could do once set free. By granting permission to ourselves for authenticity, grace is extended to both self and others, in turn allowing the overcomer to try new things, even if mistakes are made. When the standard is set at excellence—not perfection—it will allow for a more rewarding life as we serve the God of second, third, and forty-fifth chances.

It wasn't until I gave myself permission to embrace the messiness of life that I began to accept myself for who I was— flaws and all. Once I realized that I could be loved even though I was flawed I was set free; free to be me perhaps for the first time in my life. After all, if the Lord can accept me as perfectly imperfect, I should too. Come into agreement with the Lord about who you are in Him. When He created you, He created something pretty amazing. Embrace that. Embrace the perfectly imperfect you as you look past your flaws and weaknesses to your beauty and strength. Learn to see yourself—and others— the same way. Allow Jesus to heal you of this less-than-accurate thinking. You are truly worth the price that Jesus paid for you on the cross.

While you're at it, stop worrying about what others think, let go of those ridiculous, unreachable standards which only set you up for a downward cycle of failure and be free! Be free to fly and free to try! Be free to let people see the weird, wonderful, quirky you! The you which reflects the perfect One in spite of your imperfections! In Christ we learn, "Therefore if any man be in Christ, he is a new creature: old things are passed away; behold, all things are become new" (2 Corinthians 5:17, KJV). As you come out of your shell of perfection, God will reveal the possibilities and potential that await.

On your journey towards defeating perfection, don't focus exclusively on what you're doing right or wrong. Learn from your mistakes and keep moving forward. As you move forward, also learn to be satisfied with who you are in the moment as you stop striving to be something you aren't. Admit that there are many things you cannot do, but remember there are also many things you *can* do—and that being loved by your Heavenly Father is not based on your performance. It is true that He longs for your best, but He is not expecting perfection. You've got this, and He's got you!

Oh, and those things about yourself that you work so diligently to hide? You don't struggle alone. Many brothers and sisters in the Lord struggle with the issues of shopping, eating, pornography, anger, fear, relationships, even arguing with their spouses. Don't always give the socially acceptable answer of "fine" when asked how things are going. Be real, let people know you are struggling. They don't have to know every detail of your life, but be real with your answer. Learn to answer honestly when someone asks how you are doing and reply, "I could use your prayers, I've been struggling".

When we realize that everyone is walking through some trial or another, we begin to view people with a different perspective, which then allows us to see them as the Lord sees them. If we truly see them clearly, we also see their imperfections as adding to the beauty of their messy lives. Because the Lord, who created us, finds them lovely, we learn to find all those little quirks lovely as well.

You also need to love yourself in all of your glorious messiness, too. Sometimes, the grace we need to extend is to ourselves. Personally speaking, I thought I had made too many mistakes, and that my life was too much of a mess; therefore, I had to hide me. There was no way I could let people see the real me: they might not like me if they did. I didn't realize that those peculiar things about me, those flaws, could actually add to my attractiveness and make me all the more interesting.

I look at my children and I love them so much that my heart feels as if it will explode. Are they perfect? Ha! Not a chance, after all, their mom—who raised them—is a sinner and deeply flawed. Does that mean that they are unlovable? Not in a million years!!! Sometimes I love them even more because their flaws make them all the more interesting. (Okay, so sometimes I think a little more discipline administered when they were younger might have helped, too, but...it'll work out!) That's the same way our heavenly Father feels about us, too. He looks at us, sees all those flaws and loves us anyway. When He looks at us, He sees us as we can be. When you begin to look at others in the same manner, your world will open up like you've never dreamed possible. We are all sinners, yet we are all loved by the Perfect One. The gospel exemplifies this perfect love shown towards a deeply imperfect world; we too can experience that love in the midst of all our imperfections as we are perfectly loved by our Heavenly Father. The messier life gets, the more we need that love. The next time you are blessed by being allowed to see the messiness of another's life, reach out in love to them. While you're at it, reach out in love to yourself the next time your own life gets messy. Each and every overcomer is a work in progress and we need to treat ourselves as such, with that same grace and mercy as we would show towards another.

My life is messy, my house is not in perfect order, but I am allowing myself to be a work in progress. I will still invite you in to experience the messiness of life with me as I share the mistakes I am making in order that you might grow along with me. You can see my messy house. I might use my "mom voice" with my kids while you are there. We might even talk about one or two of the skeletons in our closets over coffee. The conversation just might open an entirely new level of intimacy between us as we allow each other to see more of our messiness. As you overcome this particular hurdle in life and you let others into your messy life, the stress associated with performance will lesson. Eventually, it may all disappear as you allow yourself to authentically be who you were created to be and invite others to live authentically alongside you. Life will always be messy but that only makes it more beautiful!

Perhaps if we were honest, we could admit that our greatest fear is that, if we truly allowed others to see us as we are, in all our perfect imperfectness, we may no longer be accepted, so we continue to answer with our fake "I'm fine". We continue to minimize our needs in order to preserve appearance. There may be a few more reasons why we engage in minimizing as well.

Maybe you were taught to think of yourself as *less than,* as if you have less value than another. Some may minimize in an attempt to move attention away from them. Still others may minimize due to a mistaken belief that they must always be strong for everyone else, allowing no weakness to be shown. For me, I found that I minimized because I often felt unworthy. I didn't think I deserved any one's care, because there were people who had it much worse than I did.

Dear overcomer, remind yourself who you are in Christ: you are royalty, you have authority, you are enough, and you truly do have worth. As we are reminded in Scriptures, "Fear ye not therefore, ye are of more value than many sparrows" (Matthew 10:31, KJV). The Lord cares about your struggles; stop minimizing your value and honestly say what you need. Remember to whom you belong. You matter, and God cares. Keep in mind the high price that was paid for you: "But God commendeth his love toward us, in that, while we were yet sinners, Christ died for us" (Romans 5:8, KJV). *It* isn't nothing—*it* is something because *you* are something. If you hurt, tell someone, speak up if you have a need. If you aren't fine, say so and ask for prayers. You don't have to share all the details but let people know your needs. And, on the other hand, if you don't want to talk about something, you don't have to. You are not being humble or godlier by minimizing your situation or need or by suffering in silence. If no one knows, no one can help.

When you recognize you are royalty, life as you know it changes. God paid the ultimate price for you when His Son died on the cross, because of that, you have value beyond measure. A well-known verse reminds us: "For God so loved the world that he gave his only begotten Son, that whosoever believeth in him should not perish, but have everlasting life" (John 3:16, KJV). We are so loved that we are worth the ransom price paid by Jesus on the cross: His death.

In the past, you may have minimized to remain invisible, but here, in your come-over moment in life like Esther, your purpose is being revealed:

"For if thou altogether holdest thy peace at this time, then shall there enlargement and deliverance arise to the Jews from another place; but thou and thy father's house shall be destroyed: and who knoweth whether thou art come to the kingdom for such a time as this?" (Esther 4:14, KJV).

No more hiding behind your perfect pretend life; no more false answers of "I'm fine"!

Chapter 18

Joy in the Testing

arely do we equate joy with testing, but it can happen. Joy can be found even when the fiery trials burn with greater intensity, just as joy can be found in the dry desert seasons of waiting. Joy can be found when we look for it, and look for it we must in order to make life worth living. In the most difficult moments, when we utter a sacrifice of praise, we can enjoy the sweetest flickers of joy, the kind that take your breath away.

I will be the first to admit, I'd rather learn my lessons without being tested. But life doesn't work that way; you have to experience the trials in order to gain the necessary knowledge. Tests and trials also teach us another aspect of God's character: His love towards all of us.

Here's something else to consider while in the season of testing: could all this added pressure actually be preparation for added promise? Scriptures state:

"We all experience times of testing, which is normal for every human being. But God will be faithful to you. He will screen and filter the severity, nature, and timing of every test or trial you face so that you can bear it. And each test is an opportunity to trust him more, for along with every trial God has provided for you a way of escape that will bring you out of it victoriously."(1 Corinthians 10:13, TPT)

These times of testing were normal, and they would not break me as they lead me to greater areas of breakthrough. In a way, testing is vital to our spiritual growth, as we make new discoveries about ourselves from deep within the trials.

As we seek joy in the face of testing, we also learn of a different type of bravery that is best defined by those who face unchanging circumstances or impossible odds, yet still continue to greet each day with hope and expectancy. Even while facing a dead-end job, or the monotony of a season in which nothing changes, or unending health or financial issues, you can find a way to get up each day, filled with hope, and face it with a smile. Unfortunately we tell ourselves all too often that we can't find anything to be happy about in our trials; allowing our minds to rob us of our joy. His praise can truly ever be on our lips as we purposefully seek His presence within the testing. We can find joy, perhaps not in the trial itself, but within His presence at our side, as well as within those little love notes He sends throughout the day.

We can also lessen the pressure while in the testing by relinquishing the need to remain strong all throughout our trials. There will be meltdowns and breakdowns, tears and fears. The testing will most likely be painful, but we don't have to hide it, nor do we need to present ourselves as perfect. Keep in mind that you don't have to get through the test perfectly, you just need to get through it. Allow others to see how human you are in the testing; this can actually encourage them as they learn that they are not alone in their struggles. It might even provide you with a ministry opportunity!

Here are a few of the verses that have allowed me to find joy in the testing:

"In the same way that gold and silver are refined by fire, the Lord purifies your heart by the tests and trials of life" (Proverbs 17:3, TPT).

"But he knows the way that I take; and when he has tried me, I shall come out as gold" (Job 23:10, ESV).

"Though we experience every kind of pressure, we're not crushed. At times we don't know what to do, but quitting is not an option" (2 Corinthians 4:8, TPT).

"That the trial of your faith, being much more precious than of gold that perisheth, though it be tried with fire, might be found unto praise and honour and glory at the appearing of Jesus Christ" (1 Peter 1:7, KJV)

To summarize the above Scriptures, the trials and testing will come. It isn't a matter of if, but one of when. One thing you can pin your hope on is that these testings are not always a bad thing. Oh, they may be meant for evil by the enemy, but God can turn that around and use them for your good as you are stretched in your faith.

When life goes smoothly, it's easy to believe in God and His promises, but it's when life isn't so smooth that our faith is tried and tested. I will admit that I, for one, want to come forth as gold in this testing time as I am reminded in Scriptures: "But he knoweth the way that I take: when he hath tried me, I shall come forth as gold" (Job 23:10, KJV). I wish I could tell you that I walked through this particular area of my testing with flying colors: that my attitude was always joyful and upbeat as I put my trust in the Lord, but, like most of my life, the outcome was not as expected. I will admit that there were preconceived notions as to what I imagined my behavior should be throughout these trials. I can also admit that I failed, often and repeatedly. I believed—mistakenly—that there should be no tears, no meltdowns; that through it all, I had to remain strong and courageous.

If I'm honest, many days—and I still struggle with this at times—I just wanted to walk away from God. But all of this was a test; first it was a test to be sure I wasn't going to give up on Him, but then it became a test in which I needed to learn that He wasn't giving up on me, even if the tests continued longer than I thought they should. I went through many emotions, such as anger, hatred, worthlessness; felt cheated and scared; and was ready to quit. I often felt like I was the only person on this earth for whom the promises of God did not apply. I actually questioned if I was loved—or even loveable! Where was my joy?

It was then that I realized: perhaps these were not just attacks, or even tests, but more of a stretching or conditioning. Much like a soldier drills for battle, so was I preparing for war. I was exercising my faith, becoming stronger with each trial, and increasing my personal history of God's faithfulness. I didn't understand the testing process. I failed to understand how things needed to align before prayers could come into being and be answered. I didn't understand how to trust in His perfect timing.

Nor did I understand the spiritual battles that needed to be fought and won.

I was in territory that was new to both me and my family, fighting to take back territory that had been stolen from us generations ago. I was also battling for future generational blessings. It was here on the battlefield that everything became real to me. Life and all its trials began to make sense, even began to be worth all the pain the trials brought with them. Maybe this was the first time my faith really came into play. I had never doubted my salvation, now it was time for the next level; a level that took a lot of stretching, a lot of conditioning, as well as a lot of pain.

This also prepared me to accept the additional lessons learned in the testing, and, dare I say it, showed me a glimmer of that ever-elusive joy. As I learned how these tests were helping me study for my next assignment, I was able to shift my attitude towards them. As I learned that I *would* get through them, I also learned *how* to get through them with greater ease. I began to lean into my tests as I actively sought the lessons the Lord wanted me to learn. He became my source of strength and comfort as I learned that the testing was actually for my benefit.

As difficult as it is for our finite minds to comprehend, God actually can turn around the bad in our life and use it for good as we learn from His instruction. One of the greatest lessons that I learned came when I realized how strong I was when my strength was joined with His. As my faith became real as a result of this testing, I learned that I was capable of anything He called me to because He was right there with me.

The longer it takes for your prayers to be answered, the more of a challenge it becomes to stand firm. For me, that challenge came in a hesitation to continue standing for breakthrough prayers at church. At one point, a pew friend even asked "But it's getting better, right?" How could I give her a truthful answer when it wasn't? From my perspective in the natural, life wasn't changing and I was still barely scraping by. So, that was my answer: I'm getting stronger spiritually and am eagerly waiting for the natural to catch up.

Glimmers of joy can also be found as the testing reveals hidden facets of our character, such as perseverance, resolve, or determination. You will get through the test, but how well you do is entirely up to you and your attitude. Each test will require a different set of skills; skills built upon previous strengths as you face each new test. Once you know that you can overcome these trials, they actually become easier to face, causing the enemy to have less power over you. With God at your side, you are already victorious.

As you are being tested, you will also be built up in your spirit as you learn how big your God is. Overcomers also realize that they are being refined as many impurities are being burned away as a result of the test. Due to the power that resided in you on the day of salvation, a foundation firmly built on Christ is formed out of your victories. The overcomer learns that the purpose of these tests is actually to draw them closer to their Lord, as they willingly prepare for what is to come. Pop quizzes don't cause faith to waver; instead, the overcomer remains strong—she does not faint or grow weary, and she remains steadfast. As an overcomer, you have come to the realization that the purpose of these tests are necessary in the formation of a new you.

While all of that is going on, there is another transformation also occurring. It is now time for joy as you learn who the source of your joy is. We read, "...for the joy of the Lord is your strength" (Nehemiah 8:10, KJV). There is only one source for our strength, and that is the Lord. Many overcomers need repeated lessons in this subject before they can advance, often requiring multiple sacrifices and trials, along with pain and tears, before they arrive at the conclusion that the joy of the Lord is indeed their strength.

I can remember a point, years into the testing, when I realized this had become my life verse. Not only had it been spoken over me often by various sources, it had also become true as all of my tears and trials cultivated the most amazing relationship with my Heavenly Father. I had learned to find joy in my trials; joy in who He was for me and in what He was going to do in my life. Even though it is difficult, we can praise Him while in the fire, and praise that originates from our deepest pain is unbelievably beautiful. Here you will learn that your face can shine with joy even as tears flow from your eyes. Life may remain challenging as you are continually tested, but, accompanied by the knowledge that God is by your side, you can now experience joy in the testing.

He can become your joy, a joy like nothing else you've ever know. To your great surprise, this joy can be found even as the fire burns hottest in the midst of trials, but, no matter what life

SHERRY LYNN

may throw at you, the Lord is truly on your side. Attacks from the enemy that are meant to harm you are now used by the Lord for your edification. Before you learn this truth about joy, life is gray, empty, and hopeless as you go through the motions with your only intent to get through another day. You now know that no matter what tactics the enemy may choose to employ, you possess the strength and resolve to continue on. No one can steal your joy away!

Just why is joy so important to an overcomer? First and foremost, it restores hope. It allows the individual to be encouraged regardless of the situation in which they find themselves. In the face of adversity, it allows you to continue on as you know joy can be found in Him regardless of circumstances or how you feel; making the conscious choice to put on joy daily.

For you, as an overcomer, this means you can find joy in any situation, and many times you will need to. The choice whether or not to actively seek joy resides solely in your hands, is within your power, and is entirely up to you to choose it. Joy will get you through those particularly difficult, trying times. Joy doesn't mean you will be happy about the trials, but it does mean that you can find good in the bad, the silver lining in the storm cloud.

Even when your heart is breaking, you can battle for joy. On those days when you can find little to be joyful about, start fighting for your joy. Your default answer should always be "Thank you, Lord, that when you called, I answered", because you always have Him.

The enemy is always trying to defeat you, but joy is a weapon always at your disposal. Your joy will bring confusion to the enemy as he attempts to overshadow your light with his darkness. As you release joy, you bring excitement and life. Little does he know that your joy will completely blot out his darkness. Even when it hurts, even when your heart breaks, remember: "They that sow in tears shall reap in joy" (Psalm 126:5, KJV).

Chapter 19

Why, You Beautiful Overcomer, You!

Time and again we can surprise ourselves with the extent of our capabilities when facing overwhelming trials. In the moment, we may not have the confidence to believe that we will ever get through the trials, but repeated encounters will prove otherwise. We learn those trials weren't the end of the world we thought they were. Over time, we also learn that we are overcomers, and beautiful ones at that!

Beautiful overcomers have learned to praise Him through their tears. That's right, even with tears of anguish streaming down your face, you still possess the ability to praise the Lord. It was challenging in the beginning, but now the sacrifice of praise comes much easier. We are reminded in Scriptures, "By him therefore let us offer the sacrifice of praise to God continually, that is, the fruit of our lips giving thanks to his name" (Hebrews 13:15, KJV). When we praise Him at this juncture we are showing amazing faith in God, in His promises and in the future. For the overcomer, these may prove to be some of the sweetest moments spent in His presence. You've learned to fight the enemy with your praise; in fact, it has become your greatest weapon. Look at these moments as spoils of the battle you've just fought and won.

You've also learned that you will be able to overcome whatever life throws your direction because the Lord is by your side. The enemy may send numerous assaults your way, but I am confident that you will praise the Lord; in fact, you may even begin to praise Him louder. As the overcomer you are, you have also learned to live a lifestyle of worship no matter what the time or place. It could be while driving down the road listening to a song filled with an amazing message, or while reading the Bible and finding a verse that demands you stop and listen to His still small voice as He speaks to you. Worship can take place anywhere and at any time: at work, words of praise can be quietly whispered to the Lord under your breath; in the car, prayers may be offered while driving. I'm sure you've made your own discoveries in this area by now.

Overcomers have learned to live life loved. You are His beloved; He has chosen you and called you out. Scriptures remind overcomers of this very fact: "But ye are a chosen generation, a royal priesthood, an holy nation, a peculiar people; that ye should shew forth the praises of him who hath called you out of darkness into his marvellous light" (1 Peter 2:9, KJV).

You've also learned to listen to that still, small voice within you, that voice that is as quiet as the thunder or as deafening as a whisper. You now live your life dedicated to Him as you follow His calling for who He has created you to be. You've learned to just be you, finally realizing that nothing satisfies that gaping wound buried deep within your soul but Him. By now, I'm sure that you also have your heart wide open as you have learned to be completely yourself with the Lord, creating a deeper intimacy with Him.

At this point in your journey, the chains that have been holding you back have been broken off; you can now live the life you have been created to live. As an overcomer, you are aware of satan's attempts to attack and destroy, but by now you are better equipped to fend them off. You've also discovered your values, your purpose, and your dreams, along with your strengths and passions. You walk through life with authority in Christ, knowing who you are and to whom you belong. You've also learned that you are a member of a royal family—after all, your Heavenly Father is the King—and you walk accordingly. You also walk with a supernatural confidence, knowing that everywhere you walk, Jesus accompanies you.

Because of Christ's redemptive work on the cross, overcomers also realize and make use of that resurrection power that resides within all who follow Jesus; this power allows you to experience confidence in any circumstances because your security rests firmly in Christ. Wisdom gained along the journey reminds you that, since the Lord has gotten you through trials in the past, He will continue to guide you through any and all future trials.

You've learned that peace is not the absence of problems but rather the presence of God. Life isn't a matter of *if* the trials come, but *when.* As stated in Scripture, "My brethren, count it all joy *when* ye fall into divers temptations" (James 1:2, KJV). [Emphasis mine]. Throughout the trials, you have been broken and repaired, and become stronger as a result. You've learned to find your strength in the joy of the Lord. You have also been freed from your past and the multitude of fears that have been imprisoning you; now you are free to move into your destiny. You find yourself stepping out in faith and chasing your God-given dream. The ordinary is no longer enough for you; you have hope for all the possibilities of what can be in your life as you live it for Him. You live an abundant life daily because you have closed the gap between who you want to be and who you actually are. You've discovered your place in God's design for the world as He makes use of your unique gifts and talents. People-pleasing and worrying about what others think have become actions of your pre-overcoming days. Propelled by your recent acceptance of your royalty, you no longer allow others to treat you poorly and have come to expect respect at all times. When you walk into the room, the atmosphere changes; you are a world changer and an atmosphere shifter!

The lies which once controlled your life no longer have any effect over you because you have renewed your mind as a result of being a new creation (Romans 12:2, 2 Corinthians 5:17). You have learned to think differently, about both yourself and others; as a result, you can come before the Father just as you are. There is no shame or guilt within; you are covered by the blood of Jesus. All that has proved unnecessary has been burned away in the fiery trials.

You walk like the son or daughter of the King that you are, and, as a result of this newfound identity, you enjoy a deeper, more intimate relationship with your Lord. Within the depths of your heart, He has placed an inextinguishable fire. Because you have overcome, you now seek to discover the golden potential buried deeply within others that they too might unearth their gifts and talents. Fear no longer has a hold on you; you exercise your newly-discovered courage by taking territory for the Kingdom. You now approach each battle from a position of victory. Your faith has been matured and perfected, your trust increased. You've learned the sweet victory of breakthrough after particularly trying spiritual battles. As you trust that He will let you walk on the water, you stop fighting what He is doing in your life and rest in Him. You've learned to look for confirmation of God's words all around you—your answers to prayers and question are right in front of you, and you take full advantage of it. You can relax, confidently knowing that the Lord has your life under control. It has been proven to you that Christ's blood is sufficient every healing, every battle—absolutely everything!

Your season of loss has been replaced with a season of blessing. It is in this season that you learn to trust Him in a new and exciting way as you now realize those trials were merely training grounds used to prepare you for your next assignment. You've learned that beauty can come from ashes. You've also learned to forgive—I mean really forgive—even those who do not ask for or deserve your forgiveness. You've learned to rest in the storm. In fact, you've now learned that when the storms come and you are tossed by the waves of the sea that He will provide the oxygen you need to breathe, even when the waves take you under.

You've learned that you needn't see your prayer answered in the natural to believe it is coming. The spirit of poverty that had been telling you there wouldn't be *enough* has been told to leave as you now know that your Heavenly Father will always provide for your needs. There will always be more. There will always be abundance, even in the season of lack.

Past experience has taught you that as long as the Lord is by your side, you can overcome overwhelming circumstances; now you use that knowledge to encourage and strengthen others. You've gone so far past your initial limits that you don't even remember what they were. You are incredibly strong, but it is God by your side that makes you invincible. You don't quit, and you don't back down; you stand firm, and you stay strong. In fact, you've got the enemy running scared! Claim this verse as your own: "So that we may boldly say, The Lord is my helper, and I will not fear what man shall do unto me" (Hebrew 13:6, KJV).

So, my beautiful overcomer, why don't you stand a little taller and pray a little bolder as you face this life with this brand-new strength? Know that you will make a difference wherever your journey may take you.

What are you waiting for? Let's go change the world!

Chapter 20

Stories from the Fire

In this section of the book I share the stories of overcomers who have made this journey before you in hopes of offering encouragement. No names have been used as they could be any woman's story—they could be every woman's story. You could even find yourself on either side of the story. Maybe you will see yourself in these pages; if so, I pray that you might experience total freedom in Christ's forgiveness. Then, I pray, you will forgive yourself and move forward in your life as you are freed to step into your destiny.

IT WAS A DARK AND STORMY NIGHT

Lightning flashed, thunder rolled, the rain was coming down in torrents as the woman drove the unfamiliar roads in search of internet services. She was on a deadline; her final paper for a class had been due the previous day. She was late in turning it in. She was never late.

The previous week had turned her world upside down. She had finally told her abuser she had had enough. After a ten day respite from the man and his behavior, she packed up a few personal possessions along with her children and left him. While it was what necessary at the time, here she was, homeless, jobless, trying to finish up her paper as she worked towards a degree. She was a quivering mess of emotions and she could barely function. The first night away from him, she tried to sleep on a friend's couch but every time she closed her eyes she would begin shaking; the kind of cold that no amount of blankets could warm. And the tears just wouldn't stop, pouring from her eyes with a will of their own.

The storm continued as she pulled into the parking lot of a fast food chain that was known for providing free internet. She, along with her son, ran into the building dodging the rain as best they could. She felt obligated to make a purchase before making use of their internet, so, even though money was almost nonexistent, she allowed her son to order something—there was no way she could eat a thing.

Her hands shook as she pulled out her laptop. She was stressed beyond belief and cried almost constantly. But she was determined to get this paper finished and submitted. She was so shaken by recent events that she could not function; her son had to help her with the finishing touches and the technical aspects of the submission of the paper. Her professor had suggested she skip the assignment completely; if she did she'd come out of the class with a B, but that wasn't her.

So, she did it. The paper was perfect other than a ten point deduction for lateness. She finished the class with 990/1000. Finished in spite of all that was going wrong in her life. Even though she didn't remember what she had written the papers on most of the time, she finished. Not only did she finish, she graduated with her degree. Not only did she graduate, she graduated summa cum laude. Not only did she work for one degree, she pursued another. Graduating with distinction. Graduating in spite of a life that was falling apart. Graduating in spite of those who wanted her to fail. Graduating as she became an overcomer.

HELP ME

As the woman drove home from her attorney's office she placed a call to her church requesting help in an emergency situation. Of the three pastors at the church, the one who picked up the phone was the man she was least familiar with. Barely keeping her tears in check, the woman briefly explained her desperate need for help in moving out of the house and away from her abuser within the next two days. The pastor, while sympathetic, was understandably concerned about the short time frame. Much to the woman's relief, he committed the help of other men from the church. Before the woman had made the twenty minute drive home, her phone was ringing. Indicating a call from the number she had dialed minutes ago. The same pastor was calling. Speaking to her with great concern in his voice but refusing to offer her aid, he sounded almost as devastated as she felt; he was only acting on the head pastor's decision. She thought her heart would stop. In her greatest time of need, she was being refused help by the very place that was to offer sanctuary.

Sadly, she never returned to that church. She didn't feel as if she could.

Her support system disappeared at the very moment she needed them the most. Where was God in all of this?

In that moment, the fire threatened to consume her.

But God in His grace and mercy did not allow it. I wish this woman's story had a happier ending concerning her church, but it doesn't. In time she found another church after visiting several but it was years until she felt safe and secure within a church building again. God hadn't forgotten her, and God would not let her go. His love held firm. His love healed her broken, wounded heart. His love was there for her when no one else was. His love overcame her rejection and pain.

ME, AT MY AGE?

Her dreams had begun to turn to her soon-to-be-empty nest as she dreamed of time to herself; time to pursue her interests once again. For years she had sacrificed her interests for her husband and children.

But once again, her dreams would have to be moved to the back burner. Due to the abuse, at the age of 48 she found herself starting over from scratch. She had no home, no furniture—her kids didn't even have beds because they hadn't been allowed to take them when she left. She had no future, no job, no hope.

She hadn't worked outside the home in years. Her marketable skills were behind everyone else's as she began her job search. She took whatever job she had to in order to put a roof over the head of her family. She worked low paying, demeaning, entry-level jobs. She even spent a season as a temporary employee. It was difficult; facing these mind-numbing jobs just about did her in. But she got up each day, went to work, and moved forward even if at a snail's pace. Her future hinged on finding a good job. She's still looking.

In the process, the woman has learned a great deal about herself and what she can do. After living for years in a marriage with strictly defined gender roles, she found she could buy a car. She could buy a gun. She could even learn how to buy her own house. She overcame what attempted to destroy her.

THE DAY AFTER

Still struggling with her decision of have a PFA against her husband, the woman woke on the first morning after the man had been removed from their home. There was something different about today; the house felt completely different. She wandered around the house before her children got up, still questioning her decision to get the man out of the house. The twisted lies he had turned into her truth rolled around in her head as she thought perhaps she was wrong in what she had done by making him leave. She spent time crying as she prayed to her Heavenly Father before her children awoke.

But then, her daughter walked down the stairs and she saw her as if for the first time. There was a lightness about the child.

As if a heavy burden had been lifted from her shoulders. It was as if the child could finally breathe, could finally feel safe in within the walls of her own home.

The woman hadn't realized the effect the man was having on his daughter until he was gone. She hadn't realized how much the psychological abuse was affecting her daughter until that morning.

It was in that moment that she realized she had done the right thing. The same moment she question why she hadn't done it sooner; the same moment she knew she would be okay as she overcame.

SURVIVING

She had picked up the phone on numerous occasions in a feeble attempt to ask for help in the past only to hang it back up. Once or twice, she even gathered her courage so that she was able to speak to someone, but then she reverted back to her comfortable, familiar ways of minimizing her situation.

What kept her there for so long was her commitment to her marriage vows, to a husband whose narcissistic tendencies were slowly destroying her and her children. She called to mind various sermons she had heard preached throughout the years that exhorted couples to stay together no matter what, reminding herself that she had chosen this man and now she must life out her life with him. Perhaps the main thing that kept her in her marriage so long were the threats to take her children from her, along with the threats to crush her financially. She was often reminded that she had no money, but that her spouse did. She was often told that he would use his money to destroy her in court as he took everything from her. She did her best to love him. She did her best to do things that would please him, but nothing ever did. Nothing she tried made him happy and he always found fault with her. Many times, he told her everything was her fault. In fact, he told her that so often that she came to believe it. Everything that was wrong in their marriage, in his life, was her fault. So, she began living her life like that; living a lie that kept her a prisoner in her marriage longer than it should have.

She worked so hard to hide what was going on in her home, so hard to deny what was going on, until one day she faced her fears as she used the word she had been avoiding: abuse.

Oh, he never struck her, and he often proudly reminded her of that fact, but he was destroying her in other, more subtle ways. She struggled to believe his meaningless words. After all, this was the man she had married, the man who had professed his love to her. In fact, he still said he loved her, but his actions were so far off-base. She was so confused.

Her life reached a point one day when she made the phone call, only this time, she didn't hang up. She stayed on the line; she talked to someone. In her terror that day, a woman on the other end of the phone calmed her and sent her for the PFA, a simple piece of paper that would forever alter her life. There was no going back—not that she wanted to.

She sat in the courthouse for hours waiting for the judge who would give her that piece of paper. The piece of paper that would give her relief. The piece of paper that would stop that ugly word from happening to her anymore. She was a quivering blob of emotions, barely functioning, barely holding on. While waiting for the judge, the woman thought numerous times to just go home and forget everything but something kept her there, something for which she is most thankful for.

GASLIGHTING

The woman was exhausted, from something she could not name or identify. There was something so very wrong with her life, but she had no name for it; things were just off. The woman thought she was losing her mind. Reality was twisted and confusing. The woman remembered events occurring one way, but her man often told her a different story, twisting her words around until her head spun.

For years after leaving the psychological abuse of this man, this woman still struggled with doubting her truth. Sadly, this woman still believed everything that went wrong in their marriage to have been her fault. Everything. The battle continued to rage months and months after she left the man as she still believed her failed marriage was due to something she had done.

But then, slowly, truth was revealed. As she was healed by Jesus, her mind cleared and she realized she wasn't crazy. She wasn't at fault. As she overcame, she was made new.

SUICIDE

There were times when the woman just wanted all the fiery trials of her life to end. She saw no other way out. She prayed and prayed and prayed, but it seemed as though God didn't hear her prayers, as if He didn't care about her. The woman often just wanted things to stop and the only way she saw to do this was to end her life. She began planning how to accomplish this. One day at church, the woman heard a pastor pray for the congregation. In his prayer, the pastor mentioned that there were 4-5 individuals contemplating suicide. The woman almost gasped out loud. How did he know? How could he, or anyone, possibly know?

But God knew, and He cared about the woman. On that day, the woman began to understand and realize just how very much He did love her. It truly was life-changing. Oh, on occasion, the suicidal thoughts would come back into her mind, but she learned to quickly banish them as she basked in the love of her Heavenly Father.

FINDING PURPOSE

After her divorce, the woman realized that she had completely lost her identity. For years, she had been wife, mother, or family member, and suddenly it was all gone. Added into this stage of life was the concept of being a member of the "sandwich generation" in which she found herself caring for an aging parent while finishing up the job of raising her children. Thrown on top of all that, she found herself in a stage of life in which her very womanhood came into question as she entered menopause. As the children left for their college years, the woman experienced empty nest and found herself wandering, lost and adrift without purpose in her life. If she was no longer a wife, who was she? If her children no longer needed her as much, what was she to do with her life?

What the woman didn't realize was that her identity actually had nothing to do with things she did, but, rather, her identity was based on who she was in Christ. This knowledge didn't happen overnight, but over a period of months—even years. This newfound knowledge settled the woman, grounded her.

ABORTION

She remembers lying on a hospital bed, dignity stripped away as she lay clad in the requisite hospital attire , shivering; that type of shivering that no amount of blankets could remedy as she waited for the doctor to enter the room. A kind nurse was with the woman as she waited. Waited for what seemed entirely too long, she just wanted this over. The nurse spoke softly and reassuring, asking the woman questions to help her remain calm.

She was twenty, she was madly in love, and she was pregnant. The man she was in love with sat out in the lobby waiting to take her home and she couldn't wait to go there, but first to take care of why she came here; she was waiting to have an abortion.

The doctor entered the room. She remembered he had a kind face, but he was not kind as he immediately went about the business of the day. The woman also remembers feeling shame and guilt. Feelings which would remain with her for quite some time—years, in fact.

Then, the tears began.

The woman was told by the nurse to stop crying because the doctors didn't like that. A thought to refuse briefly flitted through her mind, but she ignored it as the procedure continued and her life was forever changed, as was the life of her unborn child, a child who was never given a chance or a choice.

The woman who walked out of that medical office that day was a different one than who had walked in. Her life would never be the same. She had just thrown a life away, disposed of it as if it meant nothing. What did that say about her? What had she done?

And while her immediate problem of being pregnant might have been solved, her solution brought greater problems into her life as guilt and shame became her constant companions. Those voices in her ear that never ceased, continually reminding her of what she had done. Voices loud enough and strong enough to influence her choices and behaviors for years to come.

Until one day she found Jesus—or, rather, He found her. He was just waiting for her to answer His call, for He had been calling for some time. Even with His love it took years for those voices to be silenced. But silenced they have been as she experiences forgiveness in His presence.

Now she shares her story in hopes of encouraging other women who have walked through this particular fire. She shares His story as well, a story filled with grace and mercy, love and forgiveness. The woman encourages other women to let go of this shame and guilt, and they do. The woman also tells other women of God's mercy and grace, and the listen and believe.

The woman encourages them to share their stories in order to help other women as they become beautiful overcomers.

LAST DANCE

The man and woman stood as intimately as any lovers; toe-to-toe, nose-to-nose. But they were no longer lovers. She had come to hate him due to the psychological abuse she endured daily. Perhaps hate was too strong of a word as it implied passion; she felt nothingness towards him. That was safer.

Instead of an intimate kiss on the lips or forehead, the man screamed at her; spit splattering her face. She stood there, hiding her emotions as she calmly watched the veins throbbing in his neck, making note how his eyes spewed hatred in her direction. Instead of a romantic dance in her lover's arms, the woman feared for her safety, knowing she needed to get away from his unwarranted wrath.

In this dance, the dance of abuse, in a twisted way she led and he followed; he was in control but he followed her every attempt to get away from him.

She made the attempt to leave the room, he followed. She calmly walked through the downstairs of their home, hoping to find sanctuary away from him. But he followed. All the while, the knowledge that he was capable of killing her filled her mind, as did her thoughts for her own safety. Her outward appearance was the picture of serenity; inwardly, her mind raced furiously as she sought a haven within their home.

She realized refuge and protection could be found behind a locked door. As she headed up the stairs towards the bedroom—

the first door she thought of with a lock—she realized that room should be reserved for intimacy and continued on. Her next thought for asylum was behind the locked door of the bathroom. She coolly and serenely headed in that direction. She breathed a breath of relief as sanctuary was in sight. She had achieved her goal as she steadily made her way towards the room which held the promise of peace from her abuser.

But she had forgotten her dance partner was hot on her heels, anticipating her every move. As she gracefully spun around to close and lock the door to the bathroom, the man, as if he had practiced the move a million times, used his foot to prevent the door from closing, screaming at her all the while. Hope was crushed; no escape was evident. She tranquilly reached for her toothbrush with a barely noticeable shaking hand as he continued to berate her for some imagined slight. Her prayers were that he would soon grow tired of his tirade and merely walk away, anger spent, focusing on some new dance move. Perhaps a previously untried step that would not involve his fury.

It was in this moment that she realized their partnership was over. She could never dance with him again. Now that she knew he was capable of orchestrating her death, she could never return to the dance floor as his partner in the future.

Steps needed to be taken. Steps towards a dissolution of the partnership. Steps towards her freedom. She took those steps and she overcame.

ALCOHOL

From the woman's first drink until her last drink 13 years later, alcohol always had a strange, powerful control over her. This woman realized that if she took one sip, she was going to continue until she was drunk. Any money she had was spent on alcohol. Every night she could afford to, she went out to drink with friends. While she never felt the insatiable need to drink, alcohol was still an idol in her life. But at that point, she didn't care. Because when she drank, she was free. Free to say and be all the things that normal life did not allow.

Sadly, with the alcohol also came a lifestyle that filled the woman with great shame and guilt, as the freedom given to her by the alcohol also clouded her decision making. Until one day she woke up and decided that she was finished with drinking. Alcohol and the party lifestyle held no allure for her anymore. She was done drinking.

Looking back, the woman now knows that Jesus was calling her. At first, she didn't recognize his voice but she learned to hear His voice above all others. To this day she follows Him with a fire in her heart that is unquenchable.

And the shame and guilt that once filled here every waking moment—they have been dealt with on the cross and no longer have any power over her.

THE DARKNESS

The darkness was as a physical presence which threatened to engulf the woman.

I'm hurting, Lord—will you forget me forever?

When the darkness came, she could no longer care about any aspect of life. She was alone in the pain-filled, nothingness of the dark. It was unrelenting, it robbed her of sleep as she soaked her pillow with tears night after night, tossing and turning as rest remained elusive.

How much longer, Lord?

Regardless of her prayers, she could not break free from its debilitating presence, nor could she escape its clutches. It took life from her; it wanted her destruction.

Bring light to my eyes in this pitch-black darkness, or I will sleep the sleep of death.

She begged the Lord not to forget her. He remained faithful as He always had as she realized:

My enemies say that I have no Savior, but I know that I have one in you!

*words in italics are taken from Psalm 13, TPT

Chapter 21

Sinner's Prayer

I'm going to keep this one simple too, sweetie; the sinner's prayer has no need to be complicated. In fact, it can be as easy as ABC:

First, you need to **admit** you are a sinner in need of saving.

Second, you need to **believe** Jesus is the son of God and can save you from your sins.

Third, you need to **confess** those sins.

Your prayer can go something like this:

Heavenly Father,

I admit I am a sinner and I come to you, asking forgiveness for those sins. I acknowledge that Jesus died on the cross for my sins and rose from the grave. I believe He is your Son, and that only His death on the cross can redeem me. I ask Jesus to come into my heart and into my life. I ask you to be my Lord and Savior as I accept your free gift of salvation. Father, I willingly give my life to you and submit to your will. I ask that you come and fill me with your Holy Spirit. In Jesus' name I pray. Amen.

Welcome to the family!!!

SHERRY LYNN

ABOUT THE AUTHOR

While in the fire, Sherry Lynn Weitzel earned a Bachelor's and a Master's degree, graduating summa cum laude. She also received certification as a Life Coach from the American Association of Christian Counselors. However, it was her personal journey through the fire that best qualified her to fan the flames in the hearts of others.

Sherry pursues her dream of igniting that spark as she comes alongside her clients as a life coach, mining for the gold buried deep within and facilitating the discovery of their identity as beautiful overcomers.

When not writing, you can find her furiously knitting yet another pair of socks. She currently resides in Pennsylvania with her three cats, two children, and her mother, for whom she is caregiver.

You can connect with Sherry at:

www.sherrylynnfire.com

@sherrylynnfire on Twitter and Instagram